AUTOETHNOGRAPHY IN EARLY CHILDHOOD EDUCATION AND CARE

Autoethnography in Early Childhood Education and Care both embraces and explores autoethnography as a methodology in early childhood settings, subsequently broadening discourses within education research through a series of troubling narratives. It breaks new ground for researchers seeking to use non-conventional practices in early years research.

Drawing together research and literature from several disciplines, this unique book challenges the perception of what it means to be an early years practitioner: powerful and compelling narratives, from the author's first-hand experiences, offer both a creative and scholarly insight into the issues faced by those working in early childhood settings. This text:

- Offers insight into working with autoethnography; its purpose and methodological tensions
- Provides professionals engaged in caring relational approaches with a series of vignettes for training and further reflection
- Encourages a wider debate and discussion of core values at a critical time in early years practice and other caring professions
- Skillfully and sensitively illustrates how to adopt a creative research imagination

This book is a valuable read for practitioners, researchers, policy makers, and students working in early childhood education and care seeking to give expression to their voices through creative methodologies such as autoethnography in qualitative research.

Elizabeth Henderson has worked in education for more than thirty years in a variety of settings, both in the state and voluntary sector, from nursery through to university. Elizabeth currently works for a local authority in Scotland providing support and advice for those working in the early years sector.

AUTOETHNOGRAPHY IN EARLY CHILDHOOD EDUCATION AND CARE

Narrating the Heart of Practice

Elizabeth Henderson

Routledge
Taylor & Francis Group

LONDON AND NEW YORK

First published 2018
by Routledge
2 Park Square, Milton Park, Abingdon, Oxon OX14 4RN

and by Routledge
711 Third Avenue, New York, NY 10017

Routledge is an imprint of the Taylor & Francis Group, an informa business

British Library Cataloguing-in-Publication Data
A catalogue record for this book is available from the British Library

Library of Congress Cataloging-in-Publication Data
A catalog record for this book has been requested

ISBN: 978-1-138-73522-4 (hbk)
ISBN: 978-1-138-73523-1 (pbk)
ISBN: 978-1-315-18668-9 (ebk)

Typeset in Bembo
by codeMantra
Printed and bound by CPI Group (UK) Ltd, Croydon, CR0 4YY

CONTENTS

FOREWORD

Once in a while, we read a book that strikes at our very hearts. This book is one of those texts that speaks not only to the mind, but to the heart. The subtitle of this book is 'Narrating the heart of practice' and this is what it achieves.

So many books tell practitioners 'how to' practice: how to offer an appropriate curriculum, how to assess children, how to organise outdoor play, how to be creative, how to work with parents, how to support children with learning difficulties, how to safeguard children. Although those who work in education and care settings with young children need practical advice, they also need affirmation of their beliefs and values and their personal stories of their work.

Elizabeth Henderson has given us a book that will speak to our hearts: Her style is eloquent, shot through with passion, pain, and celebration. We are protected from nothing in Elizabeth's stories – which are raw and difficult accounts of working with young children with troubles in their lives – but from the pain comes celebration of children, their spirit, and their tenacity as souls connect.

The stories in this book scrape away at the layers of policy and speak of how things can *feel* for practitioners who are charged with enacting yet another policy that may be at odds with how best to meet young children's distinct and individual needs. Amid the debates about care and education, early intervention, inclusion, gender, achievement, safeguarding children, funding, and accountability, it is often the case that the people who work at the core of these turmoils and tensions – real people who think and feel and worry and trouble – get forgotten. This book lifts the experience of the practitioner; it shines a light on those who fulfil this important role.

Firmly grounded in current policy contexts, the stories stand alone – they speak for themselves. In addition to the stories, which should really be read first, what sets this book apart is the thorough grounding in the relevant literature on early childhood education and its methodological approach to autoethnography.

This is a rare accomplishment. As you will read towards the end of the book, the strength of a text lies in its ability to effect change. This book will change its readers; it will speak to hearts and change minds.

Aside from their families, the people who work with young children are amongst the most important in their lives: It is right that we think about how that work impacts on *their* lives and work. Elizabeth Henderson's beautiful writing style carries us through the difficult stories she has given us. They speak with honesty and hope to the heart.

Cathy Nutbrown
Professor of Education
The School of Education
The University of Sheffield
April 2017

PREFACE

This book presents seven stories drawn from my professional journey, spanning more than thirty years, working in a variety of educational settings with young children in the UK. They tell of events that changed me as a professional and my sense of identity; the "turning-point moments" (Denzin, 2014a, p. 35) of my life. Early years practitioners and women in education have, historically, been marginalised in research. "Pushed into the private, the politics of the personal is made invisible ... (becoming) private burdens unspeakable except to make their speaker inadequate" (Lewis, 1993, p. 5). Times have changed, thankfully, though there is still much to be done to raise the voice of the practitioner in early years work. This is not without its challenges, as reflected in the words of Ball (2015b) when he recently stated that "subjectivity is now a key site of political struggle" (p. 3). I believe there is no more powerful way to express the practitioner's voice than through autoethnographic narratives.

Working in early education and care today is not easy; early years contexts are places where relationships and relational spaces really matter, yet this same space is threaded with tensions. At a time when early years policies have become ever more firmly wedded to neo-liberal and economic rhetoric, 'getting it right' for children in nursery is often seen as a way to save the state from financial penalties later on. Early years practitioners are expected to comply: to work miracles on tight, shrinking budgets, to maximise adaptability to meet family needs and the requirements of working parents, to uphold children's rights, to finely attune to the needs of individual children, to nurture the most vulnerable, to meet regulatory outcomes, to close the attainment gap ... and all for the lowest wages in education.

There are many current documents about ensuring practitioners 'get it right' for every child, yet there is no document called 'Getting it right for every practitioner' leading me to believe that the well-being of practitioners is not at the forefront of policy-makers' minds. Hale-Jinks et al. (2006) suggest society is "content to let these teachers, who are mostly women, lead a career of quiet servitude" (p. 225). However, undervaluing those who work with young children is something we should contest "vigorously" (Sumsion, 2004, p. 276) and research has an important part to play, helping contribute insight into the lived experiences of practitioners. Such research is a way of speaking back to power and forms one of the reasons for writing this book.

But *how* might early years professionals express their experiences, helping to build a new, non-conventional knowledge base predicated on experience, to inform policy-makers, students, or practitioners seeking affirmation about their own practices? It is difficult for those working responsively and in relational contexts to find the time and space in which to practice reflexivity, to disentangle themselves from their context, to consider what factors are at play, and find the tools with which to do that. Furthermore, academic writing has traditionally been devoid of intimacy, emotion, embodiment, and care, inflected instead with words and concepts that purport to be objective, scientifically robust, and true. The acknowledged Cartesian mind-body split in research, and consequent marginalisation of embodiment in general, led to a historical over-privileging of cognition in research (Pelias, 2011). This has been a drawback for those working in professions that demand both emotional engagement and a responsive embodied presence. When I discovered autoethnography, I recognised that I had found a tool to help me express my voice through self-narratives and to ponder and critically reflect on the meaning of events that still troubled me, after many years. Events that had made me question who I was and who I might become. The chance to deepen my understanding of praxis, to delve into the many layers of multiple realities that had permeated my daily working life seemed like a gift, and so I began to write.

The stories in this book are not meant to convey any sort of 'truth', but offer an insider glimpse into early years practice, illustrating what it means to be a practitioner who cares for young children. It must be stated, however, that stories are not products but illustrate a path of becoming. Nor do they represent all practitioners, for practitioners do not form a homogenous group. Furthermore, they are not meant to romanticise the work of a practitioner but to illustrate the depth and complexity of one practitioner's "emotional landscape" (Sumsion, 2001, p. 195); the moral dilemmas and tensions experienced as I attempted to maintain the personal and professional values underpinning my practice, which go beyond and often resist policy constructs.

Although it can be argued that one person's experiences cannot speak for all, I have been heartened by the responses of those who have listened to my stories at conferences and elsewhere, indicating a resonance with their experiences. This forms one of the key components of autoethnography: namely, that the narratives resonate with readers, engendering a sense of authenticity, possibility, and verisimilitude. The conventions applied to positivist research are not pertinent to autoethnographic research, leading some academics to state that autoethnography is not research at all but a literary practice. Indeed it is a literary practice, but it is more than that as it straddles art and science, literature and research. It occupies an in-between space, a liminal space, a crack or fissure – an opening where the opportunity to consider human experience from a new standpoint is possible, helping build counter-narratives to the louder, noisier discourses currently in circulation in education.

Producing texts that speak of embodiment, emotion, complexity, relational spaces, and liminality in early years research is still a growing and developing field. The same words used to convey a sense of intimacy in such texts, however, also create a space infused with danger and vulnerability. They speak of deep inner thoughts that may reveal not only strengths but flaws and weaknesses too. A fear of transparency, of making the personal public and the concomitant potential of being judged by others, may be a step too far for some researchers and writers, but the importance of practitioners' self-narratives at the present time cannot be underestimated, nor can the valuable role of autoethnography in enabling this.

In writing this book, I wanted to illustrate the rawness, messiness, and joys of early years practice and to convey the potential of autoethnography as a research methodology for early years practitioners. In both the Introduction and Part III of this book, I therefore address autoethnography in more depth. These chapters are, however, meant as guidelines and suggestions. They are not meant to be prescriptive, nor are they exhaustive; a number of publications on autoethnography already fulfil this need (for in-depth guidance on autoethnography, see, for example, Denzin (2014), Spry (2011a), Chang (2009), Ellis (2004)). Essentially, this is not a 'how to' book, with answers and recipes, but it does take a broad look at some of the underlying principles of autoethnography, its assumptions and inherent challenges. With little early years autoethnographic research to date, it is my hope that this book might encourage others to try it out. Undergraduate students working on their dissertations, seasoned researchers wanting to try something new, or masters and doctoral students looking for examples of early years autoethnographic research – all can contribute to the creation of a new epistemological base, to help change the early years in positive ways. This text is therefore political in nature, for collective stories of personal struggles may reveal shared patterns of experience and therefore have the potential to be transformative.

ACKNOWLEDGEMENTS

For more than three decades in education, I have been privileged to meet and know many wonderful children and their families who enriched my daily life, giving it a deep sense of purpose. I am also grateful to the many colleagues who became friends and from whom I learned how to be a better practitioner and human being.

Coming late to academic research in my career brought its own tensions and joys. I am therefore deeply grateful to colleagues and mentors on my doctoral course for support, laughter, and encouragement, all impacting on my journey to get this book published. Special thanks to Andrea Lancaster, Jo Basford, Jools Page, and Helen Perkins.

To Jacqui Thewless, Alison Hurrell, Briony Bard, Barbara McKernan, and Sue Gleny – my generous, kind and loving friends whose gentle words and faith in me kept me positive and buoyant – I offer heartfelt thanks and love. The inclusion of haiku, written by my dear friend Jacqui Thewless, has also enriched this book. Thank you, Jacqui, for your generosity. My thanks also to Alison for her patience in proofreading my original script. Any outstanding errors are entirely my own work.

My sincere and deep thanks to Cathy Nutbrown, who acted as my *anam čara* all the way through my post-graduate studies. Thank you for your kinship, warmth, encouraging words, and for travelling with me. *Móran taing.*

Thanks also to Sarah Tuckwell, my editor, and her assistant, Lucy Stewart, at Routledge for their support and encouragement throughout the process of writing this book, keeping me on course.

To my dear husband, John, whose warm, steadfast, loving support proved to be my rock and anchor, I offer my deepest love and thanks.

My loving thoughts also go to Kaison, my grandson, who touched the earth gently and briefly during the early stages of writing this script, reminding me of the sanctity of life.

To Hannah, Heather, Krystal, Millie, and Amber – my five exuberant, inquisitive and loving little granddaughters – may this book humbly contribute to making the world a better place for you.

★ ★ ★

My thanks to several publishing houses for their permission to reproduce and publish the poetry in this book as follows:

Bashō's "The Dragonfly" from *The essential haiku: Versions of Basho, Buson & Issa, edited and with verse translations* by Robert Hass (Bloodaxe Books, 2013) is reproduced with permission of Bloodaxe Books (www.bloodaxebooks.com).

Hirshfield's "Opening the Hands Between Here and Here" from *Come thief* by Jane Hirshfield (Bloodaxe Books, 2012) is reproduced with permission of Bloodaxe Books (www.bloodaxeboks.com).

"Although the Wind Blows" from *Ten windows: How great poems transform the world* by Jane Hirshfield, compilation copyright @ 2015 by Jane Hirshfield. Used by permission of Alfred A. Knopf, an imprint of the Knopf Doubleday Publishing Group, a division of Penguin Random House LLC. All rights reserved.

"Opening the hands between here and here" from *Come, thief: Poems* by Jane Hirshfield, copyright @ 2011 by Jane Hirshfield. Used by permission of Alfred A. Knopf, an imprint of the Knopf Doubleday Publishing Group, a division of Penguin Random House LLC. All rights reserved.

Bashō's "The Dragonfly" [p. 56] from *The essential haiku: Versions of Basho, Buson and Issa, edited and with an introduction* by Robert Hass. Introduction and selection copyright © 1994 by Robert Hass. Reprinted by permission of HarperCollins Publishers.

"She introduces her baby to his shadow" by Nigel Jenkins from *Another country: Haiku poetry from Wales* edited by Jenkins, Jones and Rees, copyright @ 2011 by Nigel Jenkins. Used by kind permission of Nigel Jenkins' estate and Planet magazine (www.planctmagazinc.org.uk).

A methodology of the heart: Evoking academic and daily life by Ronald J. Pelias, copyright 2004 by AltaMira Press. Used by permission of AltaMira Press, a division of Rowman and Littlefield Publishers, Inc. All rights reserved.

INTRODUCTION

Sketching the landscape and setting the early years scene

Making their incursion into the field of Early Childhood Education and Care (ECEC) are policy imperatives and global concepts that have inextricably altered the work and identities of early years practitioners (Ball, 2003). The creation of a "social investment paradigm" (Lazzari, 2014, p. 423) through the coupling of discoveries in neuroscience with neo-liberal rhetoric on the need for a robust future workforce (Vandenbroeck, 2014) has led to the portrayal of early years work as critical, to the extent that it is being perceived as the saviour of the nation (Jensen, 2014; Moss and Petrie, 2002; Vandenbroeck, 2014) and the "salvation of society" (Osgood, 2012, p. 41). Simultaneously, an ever-widening poverty gap reveals a worrying increase in the number of children living in poverty (Kenway et al., 2015; McKendrick, 2011). With the knowledge that poverty diminishes children's learning, development, and life chances (Kenway et al., 2015, McKendrick, 2011; Wedge and Prosser, 1973) a picture emerges of an ever-increasing circle of concern for the youngest children in our society alongside a concomitant ever-expanding and demanding set of responsibilities for ECEC practitioners.

Further pressures intrude on early years work through increasing regulation and regimes of accountability (Ball, 2003, 2015, 2016), impinging on practitioners' values and the love of their work (Moyles, 2001). This is the landscape within which practitioners live and breathe: the interface of political demands, the aspirations of early years settings to perform well in inspections, the needs and demands of children and their families, and the hopes of practitioners themselves. This picture of intense and, often, untenable tensions is reflected, I argue, in the high cost of practitioner and teacher attrition in the UK (Garner, 2015), and elsewhere, expressed by Clandinin et al. (2014) as an international phenomenon. Early years settings are commonly defined as places of intimacy and caring but such a notion can "sanitise and overly simplify the emotional landscapes of these settings" (Sumsion, 2001, p. 195), which in reality can often be perceived as "sites of violence" (p. 196) by those who have invested personally in their professional identities. Consequently there is a growing need to work critically, to render the invisible forces at work more visible and to contest the lack of value and respect accorded to those who care for our youngest children (Sumsion, 2004). There is a need to speak up and out, in order to express the struggle practitioners have in trying to maintain self-care (Ball, 2015b).

Early years concerns

Within educational research, the growing interest in emotion (Kenway and Youdell, 2011; Watkins, 2011; Zembylas, 2004, 2005, 2007), caring (Taggart, 2014; Page, 2011, 2013; Page and Elfer, 2013; Vogt, 2002), relationships (Brooker, 2002; Goouch, 2009; Papatheodorou, 2009; Trevarthen, 2012), and identity (Beauchamp and Thomas, 2009; Clandinin et al., 2014; Goouch, 2010; Hobbs, 2012; Lasky, 2005; Osgood, 2012) attests to the importance of growing tensions within the field requiring further understanding to support practitioners and create a more sustainable early years workforce.

Within early years research, the concomitant growing body of empirical evidence, consequent to the increase in research on emotion and embodiment, highlights the emotional intensity inherent in both the context *and* the close relationships with young children that take place there, creating "affectively charged" settings (Elfer and Dearnley, 2007; Hargreaves, 2000; Watkins, 2011, p. 138; Zembylas, 2004). Alongside this stands a substantial body of research indicating that many early years practitioners view caring as an important part of their work *and* their identity (Forrester, 2005; Isenbarger and Zembylas, 2006; Watkins, 2011). All of this adds further complexity to the already crowded, multi-layered, and demanding landscape that is ECEC and it calls out for our attention.

An autoethnographic approach

In seeking to express my experiences as a practitioner – which involved my desire to include emotional tensions, intuitions, dreams, liminal moments, acts of resistance, loss of identity, and embodied tensions – it was imperative to identify a radical and robust research methodology strong enough to allow me to do this, and so I turned to autoethnography. As a methodology, it has a valuable role to play in helping practitioners express their lived experiences. As a sub-genre of ethnographic practices, autoethnography seeks to portray individual experiences by locating the writer centre-stage. It utilises self-narratives situating "the self within a social context" (Reed-Danahay, 1997, p. 9), building a "platform" (Denzin and Lincoln, 2011b, p. xiii) for stories of individual interactions with the world as "acts of witnessing, as testimony on behalf of others" (Pelias, 2011, p. 661).

In describing autoethnography, Ellis (2009) states:

> As an autoethnographer, I am both the author and focus of the story, the one who tells and the one who experiences, the observer and the observed, the creator and the created.
>
> *(p. 13)*

As a research tool, autoethnography can help us make sense of our lives by working reflexively on self-narratives that may, for example, express "turning-point moments" (Denzin, 2014a, p. 35). The autoethnographer then works reflexively and critically, going "back and forth" (Ellis, 1999, p. 673) from past to present, considering what was at work at the intersection of a lived life with "history, politics and culture" (Denzin, 2014a, p. 28). Autoethnography is therefore also a tool that helps reveal what Ingold (2015, p. 156) calls the process of "self-making." Using evocative narratives, the writer can share critical events that disrupted the flow of life, catalysing a change to identity, both positively and negatively.

According to Ingold (2015), the lives of animals are constrained by their form: its gifts and limitations. Human beings, on the other hand, he states, become what they are through what they do and how they act: through choices and deeds. Extending our understanding of the human condition, postmodern and post-structural writers, such as Bourdieu (1986) or Deleuze and Guattari (2013), turn our attention to the forces at work that both shape and constrain our actions – political, social, historical, and cultural. Within early years research, several applications of these theories have been put to good effect, helping practitioners reconfigure and deepen their understanding of the workplace and early years practices: Brooker's (2002) use of Bourdieu's theory of capital and her research into cultural differences and values; Osgood's (2012) use of feminist theories in understanding practitioners' narratives of their nursery experience; MacNaughton's (2005) application of Foucault to the early years practice of Australian practitioners – all explore what shapes and lives at the intersection of professional and private lives in the public domain. Autoethnography affords early years practitioners another way of exploring their practice with the chance to "re-tell(s) and re-perform(s) these life experiences" (Denzin, 2014, p. 28), as they meet and intersect with political, social, and cultural forces to illustrate a life in the making, a life *becoming*. It helps to illustrate entanglement, the complex forces at work within daily practice, both visible and invisible, and to speak straight to the heart (Pelias, 2004) – helping disrupt assumptions and more linear narratives of practice.

Insight gained through autoethnographic practices has the power to change and improve the world around us (Denzin, 2014a; Ellis, 2009), though some autoethnographers contest that narratives alone are insufficient and the use of analytic practices (Anderson, 2006) or reflexive practices (Warren, 2011) is also necessary. Adopting an "ethic of reflexive practice," (Warren, 2011, p. 139) helps to interrogate the forces at work in the narratives that shape and form practitioners. When worked on collectively, these "pedagogical histories" (p. 143) have the potential to illuminate how practitioners come to be "the kind of teacher we have ... become" (ibid). Anderson (2006) argues that adopting an analytic approach to autoethnography adds greater depth and value through contextualising and locating the biography within its social structures, as part of the quest for greater self-knowledge.

Autoethnography is still a "relatively young and contested field" (Denshire, 2014, p. 832), consequently, there are many tensions in what some describe as a "methodologically conflicting terrain" (Sparkes, 2009, p. 302). As a rapidly evolving research practice, autoethnography can take a variety of forms; however, according to Witkin (2014a), there are "two basic sub-types", which he terms "analytic and evocative" (p. 8). Although I agree that the power of narrative, when written with "soul" (Ellis, 2004, p. 99) and from the "heart" (Pelias, 2004, p. 1), can help change hearts and minds, I concur with Warren (2011) and Anderson (2006) that further contextualisation and reflexive work may help uncover the narratives that inform our practice. As Barraclough (2014) puts it, "Autoethnography is one way of writing the self into the text in both a reflexive and evocative way" (p. 367).

Developing *interpretive autoethnography* from his earlier work on interpretive biography, Denzin (2014) created a "critical, performative practice, a practice that begins with the biography of the writer and moves outward to culture, discourse, history, and ideology" (p. x). Conversely, as a text is performed, the insider experiences of the writer move towards the reader, who then ascribes the story with their meaning. Denzin defines performative or performance autoethnography as a "merger of critical pedagogy, performance ethnography, and cultural politics; the creation of texts that move from epiphanies to the sting of memory, the personal to the political, the autobiographical to the cultural, the local to the historical" (p. 25). Within this book, I have chosen to work with both analytic and evocative strands of autoethnography. Sharing not only self-narratives of "turning-point moments" (Denzin, 2014a, p. 35) in my professional life but also, using reflexive and critical practices, creating a space for discourse around what I perceive to be some of the key factors in the narratives, working out of interpretive autoethnography to illustrate the complexity of early years practice.

A research imagination

To help add a sense of coherence to the narratives, I have adopted a research imagination based on the work of social anthropologist Tim Ingold (2007), who noted that the physical landscape of the earth is etched with pathways, created across time, by people responding sensitively and reciprocally to their environment. Ingold called these pathways *wayfaring* lines. At significant points on the landscape – such as at water sites, market places, or where rivers merged – these pathways became visibly entangled, creating knots. The *wayfaring* lines (and the wayfarers), however, were not bound by entanglement in a knot but passed *through* it, continuing on their way with new knowledge as a result of their inter-actions in the knot. Consequently, the *wayfaring* lines came to signify the way-farers' inner living engagement with "the very process of the world's continual coming into being ... laying a trail of life" (p. 100).

In a later publication, Ingold (2015) stated that to "lead life is to *lay down a line*" (p. 118). Pondering on this statement and Ingold's assertion that the wayfaring line is a living, organic path, constantly responding to change and continuously in movement, it struck me that this aptly described the path of a practitioner in education; watching, listening, reflecting and responding to the children in his or her care. At critical and significant times practitioners become tangled in knots – the threat of inspection, the demands of a difficult family, dealing with inadequate budgets – effectively creating a knot between the practitioner's wayfaring line and that of others, human and non-human. The need to be reflexive, to consider and understand the complexities at work in the knot, before taking further action, becomes apparent. Kamler and Thomson (2014) define reflexivity as the practice of working critically to interrogate assumptions about self and others: "reflexive practice uses both the personal and discursive 'I'" (p. 75). Acknowledging the limitations on practitioners' time in their practice in which to ponder the intense and emotional interactions, to work reflexively, suggests to me the strong possibility they may have to suppress and internalise the knot, silently carrying it as an unresolved matter, in order to carry on working. The knot (or issue) then becomes an embodied tension, an embodied knot.

I decided to adopt Ingold's *lines* and *knots* in this book as a research imagina-tion to help guide the reader and me in our journey, together, calling the practi-tioner's pathway (in this instance, my journey) the *wayfaring line* and moments of intense internalised tension the *embodied knots*. I then extended this to include a third part to enable a critical exploration of the self-narrative.

In this book, therefore, the *wayfaring line* of the practitioner is presented first as a self-narrative. The section that immediately follows it – *embodied knots* – allows me the space in which to work reflexively, considering what the narrative meant to me then and now. The final section (of most of the narratives) is called *untangling the knots* and includes a critical exploration of the self-narratives using literature and current discourses, to consider what forces may be at work and to contextualise the stories. Table I.1 outlines the structure of writing the narratives and working with them.

In his writing on narratives in education research, Clough (2004a) indicated there were three component parts to writing: firstly there is the event itself and the telling or remembering of it, then the composition of the text through which the event is told, followed by the hermeneutic lens cast over it to elicit interpre-tation and meaning. I have melded his first two stages, worked with reflexivity in my second stage to critically reflect on the "influence of our own selves, be-ing, experience, and contexts in creating the knowledge we use and believe to be valid" (Fook, 2014, p. 124) and have added a third stage, contextualising the

TABLE I.1 Working with a research imagination

I remember, I write	Using memory work, artefacts and embodied experiences, I recall "turning-point moments" (Denzin, 2014, p. 35) and write the narratives	The wayfaring line
I think reflexively	Going "back and forth" with my autoethnographer's gaze (Ellis, 1999, p. 673), I consider what the event means to me now, what it felt like then, how it came to be, and reflect on my part	Embodied knots
I wonder critically	I place the narrative in a wider context and critically explore what was at work	Untangling the knots

narratives through discourse, to disrupt assumptions – agency, power, and habituated frameworks of practice – to develop guidelines for future action.

A word about structure

The chapters of this book have been designed to be used independently of one another and need not be read in sequence. For example, if you feel the need to further understand autoethnography as a methodology before engaging with my stories, you should now turn to Part III and Chapters 8–10. However, if you want to *experience* interpretive autoethnography, I suggest reading the stories as they unfold from Chapter 1.

The structure of the book is as follows:

Part I: Troubling narratives is a suite of stories followed by reflexive engagement and critical literature considerations.

The first collection of stories allows me to draw on frictions and challenges that illustrate conflicting discourses; working with parents/being exposed as a practitioner and parent; endeavouring to provide early intervention/fighting for funds; working with discourses on voice/at pains to digest what is heard; caring for children/consequences of embodied experiences. These stories also enable me to explore liminality and to make links to ontology, possibility, and freedom, all of which are necessary ingredients in any early years practice that seeks to empower young children's agency.

Part II: My world, your world, our embodied world is a second suite of stories followed by reflexive engagement and literature considerations.

The stories in Part II illustrate further issues of inclusion, difference, and marginalisation. These stories seek to evoke an understanding of insider experiences of living with difference, its richness and its pain. They also help to problematise education as a site for the construction of what is considered 'normal' and they are contextualised within the issue of inclusive practices in which challenges are still to be found, the greatest of which is the current delivery and conceptualisation of education itself.

The stories included in Parts I and II are drawn from my experience within education spanning over thirty years, mostly set within nursery contexts involving children aged 2–5 years, some include slightly older children. I adopt the term 'practitioner' to cover all those working within ECEC. This is not to be confused with the status of qualifications of those working with young children, but it is used as a generic term that is understood by policy makers and practitioners. At times, however, it was necessary to include the term 'manager' to differentiate from others in the nursery.

Part III: Autoethnography at work – *This section focuses* on methodological challenges, ethics, and analysis. It concludes with an autoethnographic positional narrative.

Part III allows reflection on the relevance of autoethnography as a research methodology and to discuss its application within research design, while discussing some of the inherent challenges of this methodology.

Poetry

In giving consideration to the aesthetics of this book and to the wayfaring journey, I chose to precede each story with a poem as a tool to encourage the reader to pause, albeit briefly, before entering the story. Haiku are short verses similar to Zen Koans, which are "brief teaching stories, statements, questions and dialogues" (Verducci, 2014, p. 582). Haiku, traditionally from Japan, can be used as a tool for deconstruction, to subvert "cultural certainties" and encourage the reader to "leave the meaning-making tool of the ego to its own devices" (Hass, 2013, p. 14). Its use of "image-based language invites an almost limitless freedom of interpretation" (Hirshfield, 2015, p. 56).

I have used haiku, and the slightly longer form of haibun, to encourage a quiet pause before encountering the story, to speak to the heart. Poetry can be used like a "solvent, a kind of WD-40 for the soul" and "counterbalances certitude's lead weight" (Hirshfield, 2015, p. 129). For example, the first poem, a haibun, talks of a ruined house and the consequent possibility for moonlight to stream through. As Hirshfield (2015) states, "ruin is not a condition any person willingly seeks" (p. 124), yet if a building or structure (or human being) is too solid, what can enter? In haiku and haibun tradition, "bewilderment, caprice and the unknowable are among the most faithful companions of any life" (p. 122). The poems may not speak to you directly or instantly, but may leave lingering thoughts to ponder upon. They may need time to resonate.

Messiness and limitations

An important contribution of this book is to add to a focus on ECEC research into the messy areas of early years work and to help problematise practice to gain deeper insights; the area of complexity, though under-researched, is currently growing. Of course, exploring messiness can be done theoretically, but there is, I believe, a growing need for embodied research and a deeper acknowledgment of the power of emotion and its place in practice. Disembodied research tends to sanitise text of the gnawing and unresolved issues of embodiment. Embracing embodiment, with all its inherent flaws, imparts a depth and complexity within this book necessary to disrupt and catalyse change.

The narratives situated within this book are an eclectic affair, providing a breadth of insight into one practitioner's working practices. They reflect my personal practice of 'listening' to the silence around children, wondering, going beyond what is/can be expressed through words, beyond dialogue, to the "wordless" stories that Damasio (2000, p. 188) states are natural and happen even before language. They constitute the troubling stories that remain in my heart after many years, my inner emotional landscape. The question of memory, however, is a contested area within autoethnography. As Riessman (2008, p. 8) notes in her work on narrative writing, there may be a tendency to reflect on the past and edit it to "square it with our identities in the present". All stories reflect memory's power to "remember, forget, neglect, and amplify moments in the stream of experience" (p. 29). As a counter-narrative, however, Altheide and Johnson suggest that autoethnographic writing is a "disciplined way to interrogate one's memory" (2011, p. 584) helping to elicit new thoughts and perspectives.

I have had to make decisions about which stories to include in this book and so others have been omitted. They remain unwritten and silent. I have also chosen to address several issues rather than one so, consequently, what can be experienced is the breadth of the challenge, messiness, and beauty that can happen simultaneously within one day, one week, or one month in early childhood contexts: an insider experience.

To protect the identities of those involved in the stories, all names and identifying factors have been changed. A fuller discussion of this can be found in Chapter 9 along with a discussion on ethics, a complex issue in autoethnographic research.

Although narratives tell it 'like it is,' from the perspective of the storyteller, they remain open to interpretation and multiple meanings. It must also be recognised that narratives are small, personal stories, not open to generalisation, and that the ECEC workforce is not a homogenous body. Although it is important to note the limitations of the stories in this book, I concur with Flyvbjerg's (2001) assertion that the "most minute and most concrete of details" (p. 145) within ordinary, everyday practice can be the most revealing, helping to make practice *visible* (Lenz Taguchi, 2010). As Lenz Taguchi notes, theory in general seems to have been attributed with a "higher value than embodied and practical knowing" (p. 117). This book, consequently, seeks to extend the debate in education discourses through helping develop a broader epistemological base drawn from experience, embodiment, and praxis.

Further considerations on limitation

My storytelling filters the voices of children, creating a problematic through their silence. This could not be avoided in the approach that I have taken. These are my stories – not theirs – although of course their (untold) stories are integral influences on my stories. It is therefore important here to acknowledge that when people become:

> solely objects of study, are reduced to fetishised products of professional or academic knowledge, are fixed as untroubled entities, are conceptualised only as social actors caught up in the processes of oppression, then we risk limiting not only the lives of individuals fixed in this gaze but also the possibilities of the study of … *(children)*
>
> *(Goodley, 2014, p. xiii, my insertion and italics)*

Although all the stories in this book are told from my perspective I hope I have represented the children in them with love, sensitivity, and respect. I have tried to tell 'my' stories within this spirit.

"The heart learns that stories are the truths that won't keep still"

(Pelias, 2004, p. 171)

PART I
Troubling narratives

1

WHITE RABBITS FLY KITES

Working in challenging contexts, finding liminality

Although the wind
blows terribly here,
moonlight
also leaks between the roof planks
of this ruined house

(Izumi Shikibu, tr. by Jane Hirshfield and Mariko
Aratani in *Hirshfield*, 2015, p. 124)

As he turns the corner of the path and comes into view, one of my younger colleagues suddenly announces, "Elizabeth, you need to deal with him. He's too scary!"
They all take a step back from the door, each looking busy and purposeful, trying
not to look towards the gate. Sensing fear, I reassure them it's all okay: They're safe
and nothing terrible is going to happen. Anyway… if it does, I'll deal with it!

Lola's father is a few steps away from the gate when his daughter, running
ahead of him, takes a kung-fu style leap at the gate, smashing both feet into it.
She grins. He carries on walking. I mutter, "Thank God for sturdy gates!" and
then take a deep breath while pep-talking myself into a smile.

He's a tall man, round-faced, muscular, with a clean-shaven head. Being on
the short side, I find his physical presence overbearing and his piercing blue eyes
unsettling, but I think it's his missing teeth that make him look so scary to me.
Four or five front teeth are absent. I don't know why – maybe abject poverty
and a fear of medical interventions? The dental gaps make him look so old.
He's thirty-two. Hardship, etched into a human face, is never easy to encounter.
I tremble but can't admit my fears to my team. My heartbeat's rapid and I sense a
hazy light-headedness. I gently put on my professional smile, while counting the
number of steps he has left to the door. Six, five, four, three, two …

"Hello, Ricky! How are things with you today?" I say, standing rock-still in the entrance lobby, my feet squarely placed, giving me a sense of being grounded.

Without stopping, he strides towards me and oversteps that unspecified but well-known social space between people when they converse. He skims past my right cheek and leaning into my ear, calmly whispers:

"I know where your son works on Saturdays."

He draws back and eyeballs me, awaiting a response. He knows he's in control.

I draw a sharp intake of breath as an internal conversation starts to erupt in my head: "Oh, my God! This is dangerous. My kids aren't safe!" I tremble and my mouth begins to dry. Then, I hear myself calmly saying:

"Wow, Ricky, I didn't know you were interested in gardening?"

I cock my head and smile. My nostrils widen as I take in a series of deep breaths, ensuring my smile does not fade. There is a quiet pause, and from the corner of my eye I can see my team straining to hear what's going on between Ricky and me.

"He's workin' at the garden centre, where I help out," he continues. "How long's he there for?"

"Oh… I dunno," I reply. "Young people these days … who can tell? Hopefully long enough to earn money to buy clothes and games for his Xbox!" A slightly nervous laugh escapes. I cover it with a cough. "Have you worked in gardening for long, Ricky?"

"Been there for a year."

"Do you just work weekends?" I seek important information now, as fear grasps me by the throat and my hands turn to sweating ice.

"No. Usually I work mornin's, after the kids have gone to school. Bloody ridiculous wages so I don't know how long I'll keep going ! But I was in there on Sa'urday, helping for an hour and I met your son stackin' plants out the back."

"Well, it's nice to have time to do something you like when the kids are at school," I reply, then quickly point out that Alex is arriving with his mum and needs my attention. "Could you help Lola hang up her jacket Ricky, before you go, please?"

"Make sure this little rat behaves herself and if not tell me when I come back."

"Yeah, no problem Ricky … will do." I walk towards Alex.

Lola has red, wavy hair, a sharp nose, and cold blue eyes, like her father's. They constantly monitor the room. She is the second youngest child in a family of four and quite small really for a four-and-a-half year-old; she's perhaps a bit under-nourished but that doesn't stop her from being physically aggressive when she's really angry. Ricky was in prison recently; banged up for nearly two years for aggravated assault. When he got out his partner, Maggie, left him for another man and never came back. That's the way it's been for a while now, I've been told. Just over a year ago, he started a new relationship with Gemma, and now they have a little baby called Summer. The threat of child protection proceedings had cast a shadow over Ricky's door after his release from prison, separation from Maggie, and an altercation in the local pub. Although I hardly know him, being quite new in my manager's post, I feel an empathy with something in him that hurts deeply. He's like a wounded child and yet the other women in my team are terrified of him. They always step back when he's around, making it clear to me that I must be his point-of-contact.

Ricky pushes Lola towards the coat pegs and she hangs up her jacket before running into the playroom. Ricky leaves. The team are looking at me expectantly as I grab the most senior practitioner and pull her into the disabled toilet where I tell her I've just been threatened. "I think I'll need to resign ... I'll...I'll need to speak to the Child Protection Officer at the end of today's session. My God, I'm scared, but don't tell the others!" We pause... both say, "Oh, my God" then she puts a hand on my shoulder, gives it a rub, then hugs me. Leaving the staff toilet together, I note a couple of parents looking at us enquiringly. I shrug it off. "Ooh, hot gossip!" I say aloud and we all laugh.

The playroom bustles with noise for half an hour or so, when Lola asks to use the toilet. After a few minutes, I feel uneasy at the length of time she's taking when, suddenly, the external door clicks. Can't be! We've got an internal lock by the handle and a thumb-nail lock right at the top of the door, so... how come?

The door thuds shut as I catch a glimpse of Lola through the window and see her leg it over the fence. She's running off at quite a pace.

"Maria! Quick! Come and help me! It's Lola! She's off! Come on!"

We run to the door. My proximity to it means I get out first and head for the gate. My head is exploding with panic and thoughts of Ricky and my son. What will I do if Lola gets to the road? What will Ricky do when he finds out? So much for my professional training. I'm terrified! I want to cry and scream with rage and fear, but right now I need to get to Lola.

Throughout my career, I have never contemplated a threat to my own family. I've always felt at a safe distance, but, in an instant, this has changed as terror seizes my heart making me feel physically sick. My head reels with sheer panic and confusion and I sense that the day has whizzed out of control. I feel threatened.

In desperation, I mutter, "A miracle, please. I need a miracle."

Lola disappears round the corner of the path and out of sight. I tear on, followed by my colleague. As I take the last corner, I can see Lola standing peacefully. She's looking at something I can't yet see beyond the bushes. Maria rounds the corner and I signal to her to stop and not to speak. We exchange a glance and nod. Out of breath, I slowly walk towards Lola, knowing if she runs off now, I won't catch her. I'm cautious but remind myself I can do this; I must listen, be open.

"Look!" she says, pointing with her finger and glancing towards me, then back to the garden. "Look! Look at them!"

I crouch down beside her and see two white rabbits, nibbling grass. "Two white rabbits ...?" I mutter to myself. "How?" I pause, draw breath and stifle tears of relief.

Leaning over the fence, I say with a sigh, "Aren't they beautiful, Lola?" shaking my head a little in disbelief. "Two magnificent rabbits!" I feel suspended now in time and space, not knowing what on earth will happen next but knowing that I must keep bonding with this child, listening, winning her trust and ultimately getting her safely back to nursery. But now we pause for beauty and wonder and I'll let this present moment take as long as it will.

Turning her face to look at me, she widens her eyes and, with a sound of astonishment in her voice, she says, "They ran across the path in front of me and one of them touched my leg…but it wasn't scary. He didn't mean it." She wobbles her head in disbelief and I do the same. We both give a little sigh, mine resonant with gratitude and relief.

We stand quietly for what seems like ages, watching the rabbits as they graze and hop around the garden; big balls of fluffy whiteness, peacefully nibbling, unaware they have saved me from unthinkable chaos. We keep quiet, sensing we mustn't startle them. The moment is magical.

It's October and the air's already crisp. Some of the leaves are turning bronze and gold. An autumnal breeze picks up and Lola feels it on her face. She gives a little jump and shrugs her shoulders.

"What was that?" she enquires.

"Oh, just a wee breeze," I respond.

"How come I can't see it?"

"Well … it's all around us, really. It's the air moving around us and because it moved a bit fast just now I guess you felt it more than usual. Can you hear it, too?"

We pause to listen and we hear a whirring sound; a sort of *vvvvvvVVVVvvvvv* followed by a *whooooooooooo*.

"I still can't see it," she states and I smile as I reply. "No… but if you look above your head, you can see the leaves of this wee birch tree, twirling in the wind."

I point upwards and she follows my finger.

"See, that's what the wind is doing. We can't see the wind but we can see what it does. We can hear it too and feel it on our faces."

Lola nods in agreement and turns to the birch tree several times then looks at me and touches her face. "Can you catch it?" she enquires.

"Well, sort of. I've got some kites in the nursery and if we go back in, I'll get them out and we can all go and play with the wind. The kites like to catch the wind and twirl around in it. Want to do that?"

"Yeah!" she responds.

"C'mon then! Let's go up the path." I stretch out my hand towards Lola and she takes it.

Entering the nursery, I pass my colleagues who are still a bit bewildered, anxious for me and the child. I head for the back-cupboard where I've stored the kites. I tell everyone that we're going to fly some kites in the long-garden. Children and adults mobilise themselves to join in this new fun. Lola is commander-in-control and helps me take the kites from the cupboard. Acknowledging her position of power, she grins as she helps to dish out the kites, after first selecting the one she wants.

In the garden, after a bumpy start with a few false take-offs, she pulls the kite higher and higher and for the first time, I hear Lola's laughter and catch her smile. It's a giggle really, light and tickly and her smile opens up her whole face. I sense that she feels freedom in the kites. I can see it in her body and hear it in her laughter. She whoops as the kite rises and, running backwards, shouts out, "Look. Look at it!"

This image I will hold dear in my heart for a long time because I know we are in for a bumpy ride.

Later that day, after waving off all of the children, I head for the phone to speak to the Child Protection Officer. I need advice. I need to protect my son.

★ ★ ★

Embodied knots: tension and resolution

This was a challenging story to write as it took me back to an uncomfortable moment in my career involving fear and confusion, a sudden feeling of helplessness, and moments of beauty, wonder, silence, laughter, freedom and two white rabbits which had escaped from a nearby neighbour's garden. It still troubles me and causes me emotional pain in the retelling. The story illustrates the immense tensions and repercussions of unexpected interactions with one parent and one child on one day, making visible the multiple roles and complexities of a working day in a busy nursery. But this is nursery life in the raw; it can be all of these things, in any one day.

The story also challenges constructions of practitioners, illustrating the tension between my professional-self and my mother-self, highlighting a gap between the policy discourses on working with parents and the micro reality of daily practice. The story highlights the hidden dangers and the potential for suppressed anger in relationships based on an asymmetry of power that, until the incidents in the story occurred, I had not fully consciously considered. Perhaps I had buried such thoughts in the belief that I was someone with good core values: approachable, caring, capable, ready to help parents with their task of parenting and open to children and their needs, so why would I ever feel threatened? Perhaps I was just naïve? However, in that moment when I perceived a threat to my own child, I experienced a collision between my professional self and my role as a mother. The need to protect my child became paramount and the thin veils between my many selves became porous and frayed. I lost what had been my sense of 'self' and was thrown into chaos. My interactions with Ricky woke me up sharply to the asymmetry of power in our relationship and the way in which he had turned it round, leaving *me* feeling threatened. Yet … I also have a lingering unresolved thought, that Ricky may actually have been trying to build a closer relationship with me through his intimate knowledge of my family, but my awareness of his propensity for violence coloured my perception – but I'll never know for sure.

Although the story highlights the power asymmetry between parent/practitioner and practitioner/child, it also goes beyond power asymmetry to a moment in which practitioner and child stand as equals, bringing tension into harmony and resolution, listening deeply to the child in my care. For, within what felt like the ruins of the day in the story, two white rabbits entered and performed a miracle, a moment I grasped with both hands, entering into it listening and trusting. Lola and I shared what could be called "sustained shared thinking" (Sylva et al., 2004, p. vi) defined by Sylva et al. as the moment when at least two individuals "clarify a concept, evaluate an activity, extend a narrative" (ibid) together. Lola, no longer bound by her original frame of reference, an act of resistance, running away, was entranced by the rabbits and I in turn was listening to Lola and overcoming my fears for her safety and that of my son (at the hands of her father). In effect we were "equal in the face of this ... encounter" (Conroy, 2004, p. 62); a "liminal encounter" (ibid). We both experienced a deep listening to an embryonic pulse, to what "ha(d) not yet emerged" (Hoveid and Finne, 2015, p. 77). Consequently, this led to a sensitive discussion between practitioner and child about rabbits, the wind and ultimately to a sense of freeing, for both of us, and flying kites; a door opened and we both stepped across a threshold.

2

A SILENCE LOUDER THAN WORDS

Listening, attunement and 'voice'

Opening the Hands Between Here and Here
On the dark road, only the weight of the rope.
Yet the horse is there

(Hirshfield, 2012, p. 70)

Ruby came to our nursery at a time when her family were deeply troubled and unable at times to cope. Although she had been on a child protection order, she was at home now and I worried about her safety. When I met her, she didn't speak. Ruby was selectively mute and everyone involved with her thought this was a consequence of the violence in her life. She'd witnessed stabbings in her house where the walls were covered with graffiti- resembling an underpass. The house was also the site of gang violence and punishment meted out in local drug wars. Chaos. Fear. And police raids on her home in search of heroin because her house became a drugs-shop when her dad was in prison.

3.9 million children (28%) in the UK were living in poverty in 2014–15.
(CPAG, 2017)

Child poverty is highest in London, Birmingham and Manchester where 40–47% of children live in poverty.
(End Child Poverty, 2017)

Janie, Ruby's mum, was a second-generation heroin user living on the west of Scotland on the edge of a sprawling industrial town, near a large city that had seen better days. Alone, Janie couldn't stand up to the drug gangs, so they 'borrowed' her flat, sealed up the door, and sold heroin through the letter-box for brief periods daily. At two and a half years old, Ruby knew that silence was the safest space to inhabit and I wondered whether I had any right to tempt her out of it.

Attunement is when the adult is able to tune in to babies' needs, perhaps closely observing their sounds, expressions and body language in a responsive and empathic way. Early literacy starts with attunement between parent and baby.

(Pre-Birth to Three: Scottish Government, 2010)

One day Ruby missed a nurture group session and, after a phone call, I discovered she was having all of her baby teeth removed. They were completely rotten and her mouth was at risk of infection. Janie just wasn't coping with the demands of her children and no partner. When Ruby returned, I mashed up bread in milk and she sucked it up from a bowl with a soft plastic spoon, then we got yoghurt and squashed some fruit to a pulp so that she could eat something tasty.

Ruby's silence worried me, as did her ability to acquiesce to everything and anything she was asked to do at nursery. Sometimes, I lay awake at night in the comfort of my bed, wondering if she felt it was safe to go to sleep in her house. Did she even have a bed? Did she have covers, blankets? Was she warm? I had once worked in a small rural school where a family had fled Birmingham after the father was stabbed to death in front of them in a drugs-gang feud. Their mother was an addictive gambler who eventually sold the furniture to fund horse and dog betting. The children slept on newspapers on the floor. When several staff noticed that the children brought popcorn every day for snack and lunch we contacted social services and discovered their circumstances. I thought of them as I lay awake worrying about Ruby.

Within some contexts, silence is a thing of beauty, contemplation, or reflection; it may even be considered sacred. Mystics, monks, and mothers holding their newborn babies may all revere the silence that envelops them. "My beloved is the mountains, the solitary wooded valleys ... strange islands ... the tranquil night at the approaches of dawn ... silent music..." (St. John of the Cross in Ruth, 1985). But some forms of silence hold dark secrets – Ruby knew that silence.

I met Ruby in a nursery that provided early intervention and extra support for families with challenging backgrounds. Staffing ratios were more intense than usual, often one to two, and children had the opportunity to experience stimulating environments, including the local park and woodland. A large part of our remit was to help children build self-esteem and resilience as children from Ruby's background were considered to have low self-esteem and needed to develop resilience in order to survive and cope with nursery or school and be able to learn.

The early years framework will be a central element of our approach to early intervention, not least because the early part of a child's life is a key opportunity to build resilience and to seek to prevent the appearance of problems later in life.

(Scottish Government, 2008a, p. v)

"Poverty is 'no excuse' for poor attainment". Angela Constance, Education Minister, Scotland, May 2015.

(Belgutay, 2015)

We played in small groups in the nursery garden, or in the woodland, where we cut up logs with child-sized saws and hammered nails into them to make boats, trains, and planes. Sometimes, I thought I saw Ruby smile shyly at me but she quickly looked away again; I felt she didn't want to be seen. In the woodland, she spent a lot of time quietly gathering things, like leaves and pinecones, and she loved to pile the wheelbarrow to overflowing. Was she peacefully busy, or just keeping out of everyone's way?

Six weeks after she started, we were sitting on some big logs in the woods, singing our songs and saying our finger rhymes: repetitive phrases and words that sounded funny and rhymes that simply made us giggle because they were so silly. Ruby knew them all: she listened intently and did the actions, but she never spoke. In week six, however, she whispered each word softly so that I could just barely hear her. I drew my breath in sharply and bit my tongue to avoid tears, then went through as many rhymes and songs as I could fit into the next few minutes. At the end of that day, after fulfilling the paperwork for the project and recording that Ruby had spoken for the first time, I sat in my car, unable to drive home and simply wept for Ruby.

To develop resilience, children need "Good attachments, good self-esteem, sociability, intelligences, flexible temperament, problem solving skills, positive parenting."

(Scottish Government, 2012, p. 22)

Summer came and Ruby had been with us for more than ten months when we decided to have an end-of-term picnic in the woods: bread-sticks cooked on an open fire and filled with jam, honey, or cheese. Later we toasted marshmallows and roasted bananas in tin foil on the embers of the fire. None of the children had experienced open fires before, so they were all excited and in awe of the flames. By the day's end, the children were exhausted, and we lifted each of them into the minibus to go home. As I lifted Ruby into her seat, I thought I glimpsed something on her leg, above the hem of her shorts, but said to myself, "It's nothing." I began to turn away when suddenly an intense pain gripped my stomach. A strange, tight feeling came over me. I turned back quickly and lifted Ruby down from the minibus, and out of ear-shot of the others said, "Hey, Ruby, what's happened to your leg? Can I have a look?" Of course she acquiesced, so I lifted up the right leg of her shorts to reveal a large and clearly discernible buckle mark.

"Ruby, how did that get there?" I asked quietly.

In the faintest of whispers, she made a sound which I could only discern by lip-reading at the same time as listening, "Daddy."

"Did daddy hurt you, Ruby?" I asked. She nodded.

"Did he hurt you anywhere else?" She nodded again.

Sandra, my colleague, went back to the nursery with Ruby, where we found two more buckle marks, one on her thigh and one on her back. They were clearly from an adult's belt. Ruby's dad had visited that weekend. I took Ruby back to the bus to be driven home and, after giving her a hug, I waved off all the children, and then I phoned the child protection officer.

200,000 children in England and Wales, 1,500 in Northern Ireland and 30,000 in Scotland face parental imprisonment every year.

(Barnardos, 2016)

At the end of the day, after completing all of the necessary paperwork, I sat in my car, once more, alone, broken and in tears, weeping for Ruby.

★ ★ ★

Embodied knots: listening, attunement and statutory care

Ruby's story was prompted by an artefact, a photo that she gave me as a present before she left the project. My colleague Sandra had taken it and wanted her to put it into her folder to take to her new nursery after summer, but instead she gave it to me, smiled, giggled, and then ran away to play. It's a picture of Abbie, Ruby and me sitting on the big log in the woods doing our rhymes. It captures the moment she was looking at me intently, wide-eyed, imitating my gestures perfectly, while whispering the rhymes with the same voice she used to whisper "Daddy."

The story draws attention to the dilemma of encouraging Ruby to speak. I questioned my right to do so and whether it would help her or not. It's a taken-for-granted assumption that children will be encouraged to speak and verbally interact in a nursery setting, but in Ruby's case, I needed to think this through carefully because speaking might put her in more danger. Complex situations like Ruby's require sensitive handling. Although it is undoubtedly Ruby's right to be heard, 'listening' is relational therefore defining my role as 'listener.' I felt that Ruby's situation necessitated reflection and further consideration: Without recourse to deep, sensitive 'listening', it would have been all too easy to simply incorporate Ruby into a normative model of child development that required encouraging and teaching her to speak. Consequently, the question arose in me of how to deal with Ruby, respecting her wishes and needs and how to situate and understand my role as a practitioner.

I chose to befriend and support Ruby in the way described by John O'Donohue (1997) in his book *Anam Ċara*, as a soul friend, an *anam ċara*, borne out of an understanding of the ancient Celtic tradition in which 'anam' means soul and 'ċara' means friend (p. 35). An *anam ċara* was defined as someone with whom you could entrust your secrets and worries, someone who cared for you and recognised you. In trying to resolve my tensions, I found refuge in this image and quietly waited for Ruby to show what she wanted to do. Eventually she spoke. However, on the day I noticed her buckle marks, I was thrown back into the tensions of my role, the person charged by the state to operate professionally in instances of child protection and safeguarding. Sadly, because this was on our last day together, coupled with the processes and protocols around child protection and safeguarding, I became excluded from finding out what happened next to Ruby and my relationship with her was left in a hiatus. It left me with many questions and tensions, particularly around children's 'voices' and 'listening' and how practitioners might find ways to exert their freedom within the constraints of a nursery to reach out to children and to accompany them respectfully. Ruby, after all, had responded to her situation by becoming mute. Perhaps she felt that was the safest thing to do? So, where was her power if I encouraged her to talk? This dilemma became an embodied knot for me and one that endures, today.

Unravelling the knots: listening to children's voices, encounter and becoming

The following section draws on tensions within *Chapter 1: White rabbits fly kites* and *Chapter 2: A silence louder than words* around issues of listening to young children, children's voices, and the role of practitioners in meeting children's needs respectfully.

Listening to children's voices

The concept of 'listening to children's voices,' is frequently discussed in early years work, but what does it really mean? Much of what is written to guide practitioners in their work of 'listening to children' is predicated on children's rights. These are situated within discussions of the articles of the United Nations Convention on the Rights of the Child (UNCRC) (United Nations, 1989) especially article 12 (Lansdown, 2001; Marshall, 2006), to be heard, to participate, and to be consulted in matters that affect them. Many nation-states have embedded the articles of the UNCRC within legislation, emphasising our shared responsibility to uphold the articles of the UNCRC, particularly on the issue of 'voice', on issues affecting children in the home and within professional contexts.

Current understandings of 'listening' and 'voice' have been augmented by sociological views of children as "active subjects, citizens with rights, experts in their own lives and active participants in research" (Moss, 2006, p. 17). Consequently, within workplace practice, practitioners are encouraged to help make these views manifest by sharing time and space with children while being attuned to their needs; listening. The concept of 'listening' has also been vigorously promoted by Dahlberg et al. (2007), who predicated their work on the practices of the *Reggio Emilia* schools in northern Italy. The *Reggio* approach developed a 'pedagogy of listening' that required practitioners to 'listen' to children making sense of their world through their questions and answers "without preconceived ideas of what is correct or valid" (p. 60). Inherent in this practice is a child-led pedagogy that requires sensitive, engaged adults. Such intimacy builds deep relationships between adults and children and affords children respect.

Adding to the complexity, however, on the issue of 'listening', and to a large degree underpinning it as a driver, is a commonly held view that poverty impacts on education, health, social and emotional skills (Estyn, 2014; Kidner, 2011). One key aspect of effective early years practice, to help combat the consequences of poverty, is predicated on good "adult-child verbal interaction" (Kidner, 2011, p. 7) and "listening to learners" (Estyn, 2014, p. 4) to build self-esteem. Current statistics note that 28% of children in the UK live in poverty (CPAG, 2017) highlighting the pressing need of being aware of young children and their circumstances. This is further heightened, however, when due consideration is given to statistics produced by the National Society for the Prevention of Cruelty to Children (NSPCC, 2017) that reveal a rise in the number of young children subject to child protection in all four nations of the UK (NSPCC, 2017). Bentley et al. (2017) state that between 2002 and 2016 the number of children added to child protection registers in England increased by 128%, in Wales by 85%, in Northern Ireland by 89% and in Scotland by 116% (pp. 52–56). Adding to this are the comments by Jütte et al. (2016) who note that "There are more children suffering abuse or neglect than those who are known to children's social services – we estimate that for every child subject to a child protection plan or register another eight children have suffered maltreatment" (p. 63). 'Listening to children's voices' is a complex concept that needs further consideration. It is not a simple linear practice, as Lola and Ruby's stories illustrate. And, as Fielding (2007) argues, there is the danger of presenting 'voice' as a "palliative of amplified talk, full of fun and fury, signifying very little and changing nothing" (p. 306).

This begs questions such as, 'How do we listen – with our ears, eyes, heart?' 'Can we listen intuitively too?' 'Do we listen to children's body language, their mood, gestures?' There are indeed many ways to listen but it's left to the practitioner to take responsibility for how they listen as there is no 'A to Z of listening'. As Bath (2013) clearly asserts there is currently a need for further theorising within discourses on listening.

Problematizing voice

'Listening' is a subjective experience, bound up with the values of the listener (Batchelor, 2012) and embedded within socio-cultural contexts in which what counts as children's spoken narratives are "culturally defined" (Tsai, 2007, p. 465). Narratives are often considered expressions of children's sense of self, yet as Batchelor (2012) argues there is commonly insufficient space and time given over to children or students to lead the way, impacting their ability to construct new identities and to give voice to it. Although Batchelor's research is based on her work in higher education, the notion that 'voice' is interpreted narrowly can, I argue, be applied to early years contexts too. In emphasising the need for *undefined* spaces, Batchelor stresses their creative value in helping students to feel more open to "becoming rather than to projects of production and formation" (p. 597). She terms these *undefined* spaces 'liminal' from the Latin word 'limen', meaning threshold (p. 598).

Many potentialities reside at the confluence point of the known and the unknown, at the ruptures to our habitual way of being, during moments in which we are willing to take risks, step across the threshold, reside in the crack, simply trust, lean into the wind, or dare to be spontaneous. These are the liminal moments that enter our life with great regularity but that often go unnoticed. These are the possibilities or moments of 'becoming' (Lenz Taguchi, 2010) along the wayfaring path that may not be heard or seen, that may be overlooked or ignored, through an overemphasis on reductive methodologies that lead to measurable and comparable learning outcomes in our education systems. Such prescriptive measures both threaten and impact on other more subtle ways of being and learning through their emphasis on marketable materials, defining what good practice looks like, how to repeat it *ad infinitum*, how to be a 'good' practitioner.

Sensitive listening, or "open listening" as Davies (2011, p. 120) terms it, involves letting go of control and foregrounding process over product. To ignore this, Davies adds, is a loss of potential, a turning away from the "evolution of thought and being" (p. 125). "Open listening has this double movement: one sees differently and one becomes no longer the self one was before" (p. 123). Like Davies, Batchelor (2012) draws our attention to the importance of liminal moments and their potential.

Arguing that 'voice' is currently narrowly defined and interpreted, Batchelor (2012) suggests that it needs to be viewed as a three-fold concept: "an epistemological voice, or a voice for knowing; a practical voice, or a voice for acting or doing; and an ontological voice, or a voice for being and becoming" (p. 597). The latter is overlooked in favour of what children do and what they know as listening to the ontological voice demands both "risk and opportunity" (p. 599) to explore it. For example, practitioners may find it easier to simply listen to children's opinions or concerns: 'I don't like Sara, she's too noisy,' 'I love bananas and chocolate but I don't like spaghetti.' It's also easy to listen to what children know: 'I went to the sea-life centre at the weekend and I saw a dogfish. It's a small shark.' It is much harder, however, to tune into a child's voice of becoming, their voice of possibility, their potential.

The importance of the ontological voice, the voice of being and becoming, is underlined by Batchelor who contends that every student has a "secret garden" (p. 599) that drives them to be who they want to be. Recognising the value of each individual's inner 'garden' is what led her to emphasise the importance of liminal spaces, the space between, to help maximise and build on this and for educators to create contexts in which 'voice' could be realised:

> ... to develop ontological voice by making space for being and becoming, epistemological voice by making space for thinking and ideas, and practical voice by making space for action.
>
> *(p. 605)*

A key difficulty in moving towards a pedagogy that incorporates ontological 'voice' is, I believe, partly a perceptual one which Dahlberg et al. (2007) highlight when they consider that in other cultures, such as in the far east, the importance of the hollow in the cup is seen as important as the cup itself. Reductive thinking in the UK, however, foregrounds the material and the concrete, consequently marginalising other ways of seeing and knowing. For the most part, this includes the "feminine, aesthetic, affective, creative" (Lenz Taguchi, 2010, p. 119) ways of being. This leaves us struggling here in the UK, and in other Western countries, with the burden of modernist ideas, consequently failing to incorporate and legitimise more subtle concepts and ideologies.

All of this leads Fielding (2007), who concurs with Batchelor, to assert that voice is viewed in a tame (and what I would term sanitised) and safe way. It "smacks of singularity, of presumed homogeneity, of deferential dependence on the unpredictable dispensations of those who deftly tune the acoustics of the school to the frequencies of a benign status quo" (p. 306). And, he goes on to assert the need for daring and a more radical approach if 'voice' is to give children the opportunity to be heard and to become who they want to be. Practitioners, however, are situated between competing and dissonant discourses in education that on the one hand encourage child-centred or child-led practices and on the other demand outcomes, leaving them simply "caught up in playing a game" (Basford and Bath, 2014, p. 119). Undoubtedly all of these demands create tension and a pressure on time that I believe may preclude the opportunity to consider children as unique, leading the practitioner to dominate the adult/child relationship (Hoveid and Finne, 2015). Yet, it is within this context that practitioners need to develop a feeling for what might/could be possible; to allow liminal spaces, to encourage "reimagining relationships" (p. 77) so that children's voices, in a three-fold sense, can be heard – a counter-narrative to predetermined outcomes.

Relational pedagogy, liminality, and close encounters of the small kind

If the more intimate voices of children are to be heard, a form of pedagogy that is sensitive to this practice is necessary, as well as a conceptual context in which to understand it. Describing the practitioner as one who "embark(s) on a journey" together with children, Papatheodorou (2009, p. 14) draws on the etymological roots of the term 'pedagogy' and suggests the adult role is to guide children but not to determine any particular route (p. 4). This concept bears some resemblance to my adoption of the *anam čara* mentioned earlier. A relational pedagogy recognises children as unique, thereby incorporating ontological considerations of who and what children might be[come]. It also values sensory and emotional experiences and close relationships between children and practitioners. However, it demands that practitioners set aside any "*a priori* beliefs of who the learner is or should be" (p. 11) concurring with Dahlberg et al.'s (2007) concept of a pedagogy of 'listening' without preconceptions of what counts as "correct or valid" (p. 60).

A growing number of writers recognise the need for a relational pedagogy and close, warm, encounters with young children. Goouch (2010) draws attention to:

> …moments of incidental intimacy between the teacher and one child or an infinite number of children, when the children's own discourse takes precedence, their intentions are paramount and their choices apparent, (then) an attendant aspect of the teacher's role becomes visible.
>
> *(p. 20)*

Goouch's "attendant aspect" concurs with the role of Papatheodorou's "guide" (2009, p. 4) and O'Donohue's (1997, p. 35) *anam čara*.

While Goldstein (1999) situates such encounters within a relational zone in which the adult determines what the child "might become" (p. 667), Conroy (2004) suggests practitioners need to "let things take their own course" (p. 65), requiring openness and an engagement with a "pedagogy of spontancity and of the moment" (p. 61). Conroy contends liminal moments are:

> … visible to those who are prepared to engage with its subtleties and able to move back and forth between the structured space of the classroom and the interstices at both the margins of discourse and within the heart.
>
> *(p. 74)*

As moments pregnant with possibility, Todd (2015, p. 69) describes liminal moments as "instants of living transformation, (which) make a difference to who we as students and teachers become in the process." Liminal moments also create the space for hope to be vocalised and expressed (Batchelor, 2012), for what I want to call gestational and emergent constructions of self, be[coming], and what Hoveid and Finne (2015, p. 87) recognise simply cannot "be measured."

It is important, however, to extend the debate to include a wider understanding of why sharing liminal moments with children and listening to their ontological voice is necessary and vital: Understanding helps to empower practitioners.

Postmodern and post-structural voices and choices

Adopting a postmodern stance, which challenges notions of universal truths, Dahlberg et al. (2007) situate the construction of children's self/identity within a relational context based on "encounters and dialogue" with others (p. 58). Human encounters and "relationships" (p. 59) lie at the core of a postmodern pedagogy nurturing children's sense of self and belonging. Recognising that in a postmodern world practitioners cannot rely on "universal rules and absolute truths" (p. 56), Dahlberg et al. state that practitioners must assume "responsibility for making difficult decisions" in their daily work and "moral choices" (ibid) as they strive towards understanding children as unique individuals. This means embracing uncertainty and risk while nurturing a context conducive to "construction rather than reproduction of knowledge" (ibid), to ultimately encourage and nurture children's attempts to construct their identity. This process is intensely relational and requires practitioners to open up to new ways of seeing and listening, new ways of being, while remaining finely tuned to possibility. However, this raises the question for me of whether all practitioners can and want to work like this. Do all practitioners want to experience the unknown? Can all practitioners embrace uncertainty and overcome the loss of control? What are the emotional implications and consequences of all of this for practitioners?

Naked at the threshold

Within a culture of prescriptive targets, it is indeed risky and daring (Fielding, 2007) to let go, but at stake here is the practice of listening; the authenticity of listening to children and their ontological 'voice', who and what they want to become. As Dahlberg et al. (2007) emphasised, a postmodern world demands a high level of awareness on the part of practitioners in their work with young children and an acceptance of their moral role. Yet, it is imperative to remind ourselves of the tension-ridden context within which we work.

When children are deeply engrossed in their play, they experience what Csikszentmihalyi (1991) terms 'flow' (p. 3), "optimal experience" in which everything that "keeps coming into awareness is congruent with goals, psychic energy flows effortlessly" (p. 39). Practitioners, similarly, would need to identify with their role as listeners and attendant midwives of emerging constructions of 'self', leaving no gaps or uncertainties, to experience a similar flow of consciousness with their task. However, within the messiness of nursery life, is this always possible?

Breathing on the threshold with Lola and the magic of two white rabbits helped me to find the courage to let go, be still and to listen to Lola's sensitive emergent self, captured in a moment of awe, wonder, and beauty and the mystery of an invisible wind. Standing on the threshold with Ruby, however, I trembled and quivered at the sight of the buckle marks, sensing my fears, my flaws, and my 'nakedness' at the threshold. The necessity of falling back into statutory guidelines and controls became apparent, rupturing and breaching any sense of flow and burying any ideology that celebrated the uniqueness of every child. Instead, what arose was an unending nightmare.

The question arising out of all of this for me is, 'How might we help practitioners to work sensitively with young children in a way that is balanced and avoids leaving practitioners feeling too open or vulnerable?'

3

DARREN, THE WILD BOY

Poverty and early intervention, what price?

> The dragonfly
> can't quite land
> on that blade of grass

(Bashō, 17th century poet, in Hass, 2013, p. 56)

The first day arrives and the bright green minibus stops at the foot of the path. We can all see the expectant faces of the children and one boy stands out to me, his dark mop of curly hair and cherub-like face distinguishing him from the others who are smaller and thinner. This is Darren, whose violent reputation precedes him. I know that if this project doesn't help calm him down, he won't be allowed to enter his local nursery. Labelled violent at two, where does he go from here?

I fetch Darren from the minibus and he looks dazed. The air is cold and crisp and the children are already wearing their snowsuits to keep them warm. Singing the 'Bear Hunt' song, my team walk back to the nursery garden, hand-in-hand with the children, who are entranced. I stop inside the gate and stand quietly beside Darren. He remains motionless, wide-eyed. I watch silently as he looks in wonder at all the outdoor toys: the water chute, the climbing tower, the little trikes, the sand pit full of buckets and spades, the climbing trees, the outdoor house. He seems afraid to move and somewhat overwhelmed. Taking his hand gently, I begin to walk around the nursery site, chatting as we go, introducing him to all the nooks and crannies. Finally, we arrive at the big autumnal leaf-pile at the bottom of the garden. He stands and stares, his mouth silent and open and his eyes wide. He seems mesmerised. Looking at his bright eyes, it's hard to believe that at just two and a half years old, he's seen things in his life no child should ever see.

Two girls are standing by the leaf-pile, looking, so I quickly grab a big heap of leaves and scatter them over their heads like a shower. They immediately giggle and imitate me. Darren watches, without moving. We continue to play and eventually he joins in, throwing leaves everywhere. Then, pushing one of the two-year-old girls into the heap, he aggressively rubs leaves across her face and in her eyes. She kicks him, he kicks her back and I, spontaneously, hoist a massive pile of leaves, calling, "Watch out! Here comes a leaf-storm!" As all three emerge from the leaf pile, they throw leaves over me and then each other. Darren stops suddenly and looks at me quizzically as if to say, "Is this really okay?" He's checking the boundaries. I didn't shout at him. I didn't reprimand him. I didn't get angry. I just played. Then, I laugh and we continue throwing leaves and rolling in them before moving on.

★ ★ ★

Robbie worked in the same town as me and we had often met at meetings to discuss individual families who needed extra support. We both had a lot of respect for one another and shared a sort of professional synergy that enabled meetings to flow, to be productive. He was a very calm, caring, affable guy who had worked in social work for many years, leading a big team. Everyone trusted Robbie: his gut feelings, his insight, his worries. I therefore felt concerned one day when he appeared unusually quiet and pale at our meeting so, as we walked towards the carpark, I enquired how he was feeling:

"I'm not sleeping," he replies, "too much to worry about. Budget cuts, staff shortages, staff on sick leave with stress and exhaustion and a new boss who is … well … unsociable and bullish." He pauses, and then gives a sigh.

"I'm sorry, Robbie. I know we're all struggling with cutbacks, but I imagine it's really critical for…"

"Last week was the week from hell," he interrupts. "You just can't imagine … I can barely put it into words!" He pauses and turns away to light a cigarette with trembling hands before continuing, "We got access to a household after neighbours reported hearing a baby screaming almost non-stop. We'd been concerned about the family for a while and when we got in … I mean after the police broke the door down … we found mum on the sofa, almost comatose on drugs, with a black eye, a cut to her forehead and the baby in a cardboard box – screaming, dehydrated, emaciated, stinking, shivering. We had to rush the baby to hospital. I thought she might die." His voice breaks. "Can you imagine? The press would have had a field day! Bastards! So, I've had it now. I'm finished … not coping, not sleeping and I don't have the money or staff to deal with the babies coming out of hospital over the next few months to heroin-addicted mums. How are we supposed to support these families, on no money? Does anybody give a damn? I didn't come into this job to leave families struggling like this. Christ! The whole department is falling apart at the seams, we're going to hell. It's all going to hell. And now Chrissie, my wife, has suggested I take early retirement next time the chance comes round, before I have a heart attack!"

The rain laconically drifts across the darkened carpark as the first cold winter wind begins to nip. I stand in silence, lost for words, deeply worried for Robbie. We hug, and then Robbie leaves to attend yet another meeting about budgets.

In the weeks that followed, I felt enraged by a sense of social injustice that wouldn't go away. It haunted me and I began to lose sleep, often waking at three o'clock in the morning, feeling anguished about the future of these children and the unfairness of their lot. Did I really belong to such an uncaring society? Somehow, knowing about these children meant I couldn't let go of them. That was more than two years ago now. It took that long to get the funding and the go-ahead for an early intervention project for under-threes, giving the children what I considered to be a fairer start in life – the feeling of being nurtured and safe and the chance to experience awe and wonder. Or ... was I just being romantic, middle class, a 'do-gooder'?

★ ★ ★

Several weeks before the start of the project, we call an interdisciplinary team meeting with social care colleagues, local council fund-holders, charitable fund-holder representatives, and myself, to go over final details.

As I begin the meeting, pouring tea and offering round a plate of biscuits with the agenda, I say, "Thanks for taking the time to come here this afternoon." Then I sit down and begin an appraisal of what still has to be done. I have the habit of being over-enthusiastic about life and am used to people taking a moment to recover from my intensity but, today, the silence seems strange. So I wait for a bit. Slowly, a sense of unease begins to creep through me.

"Okay, what's up?" I enquire, breaking the silence.

"Well, we've reconsidered the grant we offered you for this project," states one fund-holder, "and we feel certain other projects will give us the outcomes we want, so we want to withdraw our offer of funds."

"What?" I gasp, "You can't be serious! Everything's in place and we're almost ready to go!" My heart begins to race and my head starts to spin. It is as if I can feel my blood pressure soaring. "But why now?" I ask, as my hands shake and I fight back tears. I glance at Robbie, he looks away.

One fund-holder representative, his pale face jaded with years of responsibility, and too little money to meet the needs of the children in our area, stares at me, detached. His hands clutch the invisible purse-strings safely in his lap as he begins to speak:

Okay. This is an exciting project and you are undoubtedly very enthusiastic but, after discussion, we have agreed that it simply won't work. What *is* the point of you taking these young children from a life of hell to show them a glimpse of paradise in the woods then return them home again? What's that *actually* going to achieve?

I shudder and grasp the table in an effort to maintain my balance, and then draw in a long breath and contemplate how I might best respond. Echoes of other meetings rush through my mind: fighting my corner to initiate this work; fighting for funding at so many different levels, bidding for grants; images of the children's names drafted on paper as our first possible group … and on and on it goes. Then, suddenly, the words burst out of me, cutting the fog:

"So, what gives you the right to deny them this opportunity? Just because they were born in hell, it doesn't mean they have to stay there! They deserve the chance to experience something different, like anybody else. Don't they?" I'm suddenly embarrassed and aghast at my outburst and boldness and I wonder if I've blown it. I breathe out and pause before quickly composing myself. With a modicum of decorum, I continue:

"Most current research shows that early intervention pays off, saving money later on, so what do you stand to lose by taking the risk? Apparently, for every pound you invest in early intervention, you save seven pounds later on." I scan my mind for the right statistics and hope for the best. I would have reread my files and papers had I thought I was going to have to fight for this damned money all over again, today. "There's a study in America I believe, by somebody called Heckman, which I've just heard about," I continue. "Heckman highlights these savings. But … anyway, don't these kids, more than anybody else, deserve a chance?"

I hold my breath during the long pause that follows, biting my tongue to hold back tears and further outbursts, as one fund-holder turns to another. Mutters and whispers inhabit the room like slowly dispersing mist before the council spokesman turns at last and says, "Okay. Okay, you can have the money, but for one year only and we need outcomes. You need to prove this works!"

But what was up with Robbie? They'd broken the news to him in the carpark before the meeting and his boss had warned him to say nothing. Of course, being Robbie, he later apologised profusely.

★ ★ ★

Darren walks over to the big wooden water-chutes in the garden, joining some other children who are racing little boats, shells, leaves, and plastic ducks from top-to-bottom. I watch him scream with laughter and excitement, finally falling over in a fit of giggles, the water buckets still in his hands. As I help him pick up the buckets, we bump heads and, for a moment, he stops and looks straight into my eyes. What does he want? I feel the question in his gaze and warmly smile back in response, and then listen as my inner thoughts spontaneously arise. "Yes, I can see you. I *can* see you. It's going to be okay." Some heartbeats pass as we acknowledge this in silence. Then, moments later, Darren runs back to the water chute, laughing.

★ ★ ★

Sitting in my car before driving home from nursery that day, I take my notebook from my bag and in a fiery, tear-filled rage, I write:

Darren the wild boy often bit children.
Darren trashed the nursery room and then he ran amok.
Darren's first protection order is like a first tattoo;
marking, etching and defining,
his life chances at two.
I AM ANGRY.
CAN YOU HEAR ME?

★ ★ ★

Three weeks later

Running up the path, Darren launches himself into my arms and hugs me, then runs into the garden to play. It's a fine day and the air is unusually warm for this time of year. Later – from a distance – I notice him lying down in the long grass stroking it from side to side. He is being very gentle; first he parts the grass and then flattens it to one side. He slowly lifts his hand and watches as the grass springs up again. He seems wistful, far, far away in his thoughts and repeats the action over and over again. Eventually, and slowly, I walk over to be nearer him and noticing me, he turns and says:

"Sometimes mummy lies down a lot. Sometimes she doesn't get up." He strokes the grass again and lets it spring up. "But I'm not ill and I can stand as tall as that tree. I'm just like the big tree!" Running to the big tree at the bottom of the garden, he throws his arms around it, smiles and hugs it.

Darren's mum sleeps for long periods of time on the sofa. Recently she escaped a violent partner, but still struggles with addiction and depression. Having moved to the city with her partner some years ago, she is now alone and far away from her family, and their support.

★ ★ ★

Embodied knots: early intervention, love, and external pressures

Darren stole my heart. Something happened when we met. I'm no poet, but this scrap of a poem, which I still have, precipitated this story. Darren changed beyond recognition after a couple of weeks with us and went on to get a place in the local nursery the following academic year. But I began to wonder whether I had helped Darren to be Darren or simply normalised him to take his place in the schooling system along with his peers. I hadn't been able to change his circumstances, so had I shown him 'a glimpse of paradise' while returning him to 'hell' or not? The words of those fund-holders still ring in my ears, haunting and teasing me because I don't actually know that what I did helped Darren in the long run, yet I know it was the right thing to do at that time and I firmly believed it then. Darren changed and began to cope with life and enjoy his time with others. His violent behaviour disappeared and he seemed more at peace with himself. At the time, I felt very fulfilled in my work, that something 'good' had been achieved, yet more questions than answers were eventually generated as a consequence of my work and I felt unsure and hesitant. I needed to find a way to better understand what I was doing, to be better informed, to underpin my work with greater conviction.

I was left troubled by the fact that funding for such intervention is piecemeal and competitive, with several organisations pitting their projects against one another for the funds to exist, for a year or so. Help, on an ad hoc basis for young children, is a perpetual part of local and national policy, but is this acceptable? And early intervention is a mercurial beast, like a two-sided Janus figure, and it concerns me.

The story of Darren makes visible the lines of tension within early intervention work and raises many questions about the efficacy of such work and the political discourses and assumptions embedded in such a policy. It also illustrates the power of context, and the possibility for transformational change that can take place in the early years of a young child's life. The story also offers insight on the intentional actions of practitioners and their unwitting engagement in discourses, of which they are unaware.

Intervention work today is accepted as standard practice in the UK, more commonly referred to currently as 'closing the attainment gap.' In other nation states, for example, it finds its expression in policies such as 'No Child Left Behind' in the US. Intervention is here to stay, but are we adopting the sort of intervention that sets children free to be who they want and need to be, or are we simply further conditioning them to take their place within society? After all, intervention doesn't create a truly level playing field for all children in a society that is essentially stratified and favours those families that are wealthier and more socially connected. Yet, the issue of an unfair start in life needs to be addressed in whatever way is manageable, now.

Unravelling knots: early intervention, poverty, and opportunity

The vital early years

The question of early intervention, its purpose, value, and application, currently forms part of a controversial debate within education. Some writers contest its efficacy and view it as a form of governance and control (Ecclestone and Brunila, 2015; Ecclestone and Lewis, 2014; Gillies, 2011); others laud it as a necessary way for nation states to build strength and a competitive future (Heckman et al., 2010); some claim it reduces disadvantage wrought by social and environmental factors on young children (Chowdry and Oppenheim, 2015; Geddes et al., 2011; Nores and Barnett, 2010). Within Scotland, where I now live and work, the Government clearly signalled its intention to pursue and support an early intervention agenda consequent to an increase in the number of children in need of protection, which had doubled in the five years prior to a 2004 review of the system used to help such children (Scottish Executive, 2004b). A series of Government papers from 2001 to the present, view the children of Scotland as our most important asset:

> Our children are our future. That is why we have committed ourselves to creating a Scotland in which every child matters, where every child, regardless of their family background, has the best possible start in life.
> *(Scottish Executive, 2001, p. 2)*

The above report also clearly noted that an unacceptable number of Scotland's children were living in poverty with one-in-ten living in households that were considered to be "multiply deprived" (p. 13) through poor housing, low income, and overcrowding. Some thirty years earlier, as an undergraduate student, I read Wedge and Prosser's (1973) publication 'Born to Fail?' in which they raised the issue of academic disadvantage for children from poorer backgrounds – seemingly little had changed since then and consequently the government pledged to fight for equality of opportunity for all children, especially those who were looked-after in care. By 2008, the Scottish Government had declared its intention to pursue an early intervention and *prevention* agenda (Scottish Government, 2008b, p. 1) as an integral way forward. In part, this was due to an OECD report (Organisation for Economic Development) in 2007 that reiterated the findings of a Scottish Inspectorate report (HMIE, 2006) from the previous year. The OECD report identified shortcomings in the Scottish education system that "progressively excluded" the weaker pupils who commonly came from poorer backgrounds (OECD, 2007, p. 71). The government recognised the links between poverty, a lack of parenting skills, and poor outcomes for children in school and sought to address this through prevention by helping children build resilience and by providing support prior to a crisis arising (Scottish Government, 2008a, p. 4). By 2011, early intervention and prevention had become the "heart" of the *Early Years Framework* (Scottish Government, 2011, p. 1) in an attempt to "maximize positive opportunities for children to have the best start in life" (ibid).

The Scottish Government and the Poverty Truth Commission (2015) recently published worrying statistics noting that 14% of Scotland's children lived in relative poverty between 2013 and 2014 and, after housing costs were accounted for, 22% lived in relative poverty. (Relative poverty is defined as a household living on less than 60% of the UK median income.) This picture is further aggravated by statistics shared by the Child Poverty Action Group (CPAG) (2015), which propose that the number of children living in poverty will increase, consequent to changes in tax and benefits systems by the current UK Government, by a further 3.6–4.3 million by 2020. Recently, more money has been promised to tackle the acknowledged attainment gap between children from poorer backgrounds and those better off. The role of early intervention is therefore of paramount importance in addressing these inequities in society, but how has this all come about? What is the background to intervention work? Below I explore how intervention work has become the norm in early years practice in Scotland, a matter reflected in many other nation states and their policies.

Historic echoes

Rescuing young children from poverty, inequality, and social ills is nothing new in Scottish education. It dates back to Robert Owen's nursery school in New Lanark, Scotland, in 1816 (Bertram and Pascal, 2002) in which Owen sought to provide education for young children to enable their parents to work their way out of poverty. Owen viewed early education as an "interventionist, compensatory" (p. 7) strategy that could help redress the balance by providing opportunities through education to under-privileged children. He also believed that the route out of poverty lay in work, but this necessitated childcare if mothers were to work alongside their husbands in Owen's mills; subsequently, his nursery was the first to open in Scotland. Compensatory provision, to alleviate the hardship experienced by poor families, became something of the order of the day throughout the next century for many philanthropists, some of whom were the pioneers of early education provision both here in the UK and abroad. Pestalozzi in Switzerland and Froebel in Germany invested their time and efforts in providing gardens for young children by way of compensation. Froebel viewed nature as a "great healer in the midst of disease and squalor" (Joyce, 2012, p. 79). Similarly, in England, the open-air nurseries of Margaret McMillan provided fresh air, food, space to play, and bathing facilities for children living in squalor (McMillan, 1930). McMillan viewed the garden as a central feature in the "reform of poverty" (Joyce, 2012, p. 79) and situated it within the slum housing of the city.

Later attempts to utilise compensatory programmes within education came in the form of Educational Priority Areas (EPAs) in the late 1960s, consequent to translating social science theories into public policy after the Plowden Report (Banting, 1985). This attempt, however, was short-lived due to a lack of political appetite for change and insufficient research to add weight to the suggestion that compensatory programmes were worthwhile. By the 1990s, a change in perception about poverty meant it was seen as a more complex issue that necessitated helping whole families. The notion that work was the route out of poverty regained attention in the early 2000s when the OECD stated that working mothers could help families out of poverty (OECD, 2006) and early intervention helped children to be successful at school. However, the Child Poverty Action Group

(2015) currently contests this notion as only a partial truth: 64% of children living in relative poverty live in a household in which one adult is employed. The implication is that work has to be well-paid in order to impact on poverty.

Since 2008, the Scottish Government, and governments of other nations, have promoted the notion that early intervention saves money through helping to alleviate the social ills of society such as crime, substance misuse, and unemployment (Scottish Government, 2008b, p. 8). What makes this current rhetoric compelling and more urgent than previous notions of the need for change and compensatory interventions is the economic rhetoric that is seamlessly wedded to the discourse on social and democratic rights, presented as common sense policy-making. A brief archaeological foray into relevant documents and discourses reveals how this came to be.

Poverty and economics

Within several Scottish Government documents since 2008, such as Early Years and Early Intervention (Scottish Government, 2008a) and The Early Years Framework (Scottish Government 2008b) clear reference has been made to the economic benefits of early intervention and conversely, the cost of failure when things go wrong. Citing the cost of failure as £200,000 per year, based on the cost of placing a teenager in a secure unit and further costs to healthcare and the judiciary through crime later in life (Scottish Government, 2008b), the government incorporated early intervention as a logical step to a better society into their policy-making. They alluded to the work of the American economist James Heckman, who provided an equation and a sound economic case for the return on early years investment, compared to investing similarly further up the schooling ladder. The government presented this economic rhetoric as neutral knowledge, with the assumption that most people in society would acknowledge it as common-sense and logical, therefore making the adoption of early intervention practical and seamless. As Gillies (2011, p. 186) points out, it is difficult to argue against rhetoric that emphasises enhancing the well-being of children and the impact on the "social good." So, is there an issue of concern here?

Heckman's work is based on a longitudinal study known as the High Scope Perry Preschool project that began in the US in the 1960s. One hundred and twenty-three children, considered to be at risk of failing in school through poverty, were given access to either nursery education that encouraged active learning and child-led activity, traditional nursery facilities, or a group based on didactic methods (Schweinhart, 2013). Their progress has been followed for more than fifty years. The conclusion of the research indicated that those in the active learning group, using child-led practices, were less likely later in life to be involved in crime or antisocial behaviour and more likely to be committed to their schooling, employment, and a more settled lifestyle. Although further studies have also generated similar outcomes, larger projects have not. It is important to note here, however, that Schweinhart considers certain factors to be paramount in intervention work: (i) the qualification of teachers, (ii) parental involvement and (iii) an appropriate curriculum, and suggests these factors have not always been adhered to on other research projects. The efficacy of the original project, however, indicated a saving to the nation on crime statistics alone for males, suggesting 41% less in crime costs to the taxpayer per person involved in the programme, over their lifetime, compared to those in the control groups.

The advantages for social and economic outcomes have been grasped by governments across the world seeking to reduce costs and benefit from a more socially adjusted populace. As Schweinhart (2013, p. 407) indicates, the research concludes that:

> ... high-quality preschool programs for young children living in poverty contribute to their intellectual and social development in childhood and their school success, economic performance, and reduced commission of crime in adulthood. This study confirms that the long-term effects are lifetime effects.

He urges that we should "do what we know how to do to prevent poverty from being a malevolent birthright handed down from generation to generation by the very schooling established to overcome it" (ibid). Indeed, I am sure every practitioner working with young children would subscribe to his words.

With high poverty rates in the UK and worrying statistics elsewhere in Europe, reaching up to 42% in some eastern European countries (Leseman and Slot, 2014, p. 315), there is a sense of urgency to intervene. Chowdry and Oppenheim (2015) argue that early intervention is a "smart and realistic choice for using ever scarcer public money" (p. 8), targeting and supporting those most at risk who would otherwise generate an annual cost of £17 billion on later social and mental health problems in England and Wales. Early intervention is, they state, necessary to prevent "harmful and costly long-term outcomes" (ibid).

The adoption of such a view, however, leads Vandenbroeck (2014) to caution that this diminishes the appreciation of ECEC as a holistic concept (p. 2). Further, when coupled with advances in neuroscience that have become embedded within educational discourses, leading to an "economic brain argument" (ibid), it seriously impinges on the concept of care and its place within early years education (see discursive space after *Listening to Lola* in Chapter 4). It also leans towards the notion that children are a docile group waiting to be led and usurps the key premise of the High Scope project based on *active* learning, which, as Schweinhart (2013) indicated, should build self-esteem, responsibility, and independent thinking. Consequent to viewing children as vital to the future economic success of a nation, there has been a tendency to conflate early intervention with prescriptive resources and passive learning, which has helped to situate it within a controversial arena of academic debate.

Intervention and normalisation

The development of a "permanent sense of anxiety" (Furedi, 2006, p. 117) within society, fuelled by a "hyperbole of paedophilia, child abuse, child pornography, childhood criminality ... (and) educational standards" (James et al., 1998, p. 197) has created the perception that children are 'vulnerable' and 'at risk.' Consequently, since the 1990s, there has been a growing emphasis on the importance of developing resilience understood to be an aspect of social and emotional skills, which help to protect from adversity. A plethora of prescribed programmes, heavily influenced by positive psychology and targeted at schools, introduced a "systematic, structured approach" (Ecclestone and Lewis, 2014, p. 201) to learning new behaviours and terminology to combat perceived threats to well-being. Some writers argue that these programmes create "desirable citizens" (p. 203) through their endorsement of "proper feelings and emotional management" (Ecclestone and Brunila, 2015, p. 15), while others highlight the exclusion of a pedagogically acceptable language with which challenging young boys might describe their encounters with fear and real violence (Gillies, 2011). All the while the root causes of inequality remain unchanged (Ecclestone and Hayes, 2009) and reflect Adams' (2015, p. 5) assertion that neoliberalism has spawned a position "not of relationships but of audit; the defining feature speaks of cost not worth."

One key element to note, often masked by the economic rhetoric, is the necessity to empower local communities through the inclusion of families in intervention work to enable intervention for resilience to progress beyond "emotional regulation and control" (Ecclestone and Lewis, 2014, p. 204). This is especially pertinent to immigrant communities in order to avoid a clash of cultural values and thereby, by inference, exclusion (Leseman and Slot, 2014). Collaborative work with families gives them their 'voice' and builds positive relationships "founded on mutual trust, shared values and a common purpose" (Cottle and Alexander, 2014, p. 654). However, this also places further responsibility on the shoulders of teachers and practitioners to become "cultural brokers and mediators" (ibid), one more piece of an ever increasing jigsaw of responsibility in which practitioners need more training and support if they are to deliver meaningful services.

Intervention programmes are often based on nurturing and improving literacy skills, a necessary factor to close the acknowledged attainment gap statistics predicated on the knowledge that children from wealthier backgrounds come to nursery with better language skills. However, there is also another view that recognises that children in disadvantaged areas have little suitable space to play, such as in natural and wooded areas (McKendrick, 2011) and have fewer opportunities "to experiment, make mistakes, learn by trial and error, refocus, reframe in ways from which people can benefit" (Smyth and McInerney, 2014, p. 291). Limitations wrought through poverty, although "culturally formed," are also "sustained" through habit and example (ibid). It follows then that children from deprived backgrounds need to enhance their "cultural capacity" (p. 292), to break new ground in order to get on, and they need real-life experience in which to do this. I believe outdoor spaces offer young children opportunity and possibility as a form of intervention, distinct from prescriptive programmes and view the lack of such provision as perhaps another consequence of the over-privileging of academic performance in education, which I noted in the introduction to this book.

When Goleman (1996) developed his concept of emotional intelligence, he considered the best time to intervene in order to maximise the impact on a child's development was as early as possible, pointing to "windows" (p. 227) of opportunity through the development of the brain's architecture. Turning to early childhood, he noted the importance of the role of the senses as distinct from other later phases of learning and development and this notion accords with many early years writers who acknowledge that young children learn best through activity and the engagement of their senses (Trevarthen, 2012; Piaget, 1971). Interventions that create an opportunity for children to socially construct new pathways, a new sense of self, through experiencing different environments through their senses can, I believe, help nurture self-esteem that lies at the heart of young children's development, their being, and becoming.

A pedagogy of possibility?

When children were asked what they most liked to do at nursery, they put outdoor play at the top of their priority list (Aasen et al., 2009; White, 2008). Similarly, in recent research on children's well-being involving 250 children aged eight to thirteen in the UK, Spain, and Sweden, the unanimous response to the question what makes a "good day" included "being outdoors and having fun." (Ipsos MORI and Nairn, 2011, p. 24). Why might that be? Does the outdoor environment offer children something special?

Gibson (1986) coined the term "affordances" (p. 127) to describe what an environment might offer to its user. He went on to argue that children perceive their environment through their senses with a perception that is not finite, but is alive, changing, and always evolving. Asserting that children perceive the world holistically, but note "invariants" (p. 271) or differences, he went on to state that knowledge about the environment is an "extension of perceiving" (p. 253) what an environment has to offer them. Perhaps this goes some way to understanding why children love the outdoors: Because they perceive it offers them something different, something more? Yet, the impact of the outdoor environment on children from disadvantaged backgrounds, having little "access to natural or wooded areas for play" (McKendrick, 2011, p. 127) is underestimated. I believe it affords them the possibility for self-development, as I discuss later.

Moving, living bodies

There is broad agreement among many writers that the outdoor environment affords children the opportunity to develop a physical prowess that is conducive to enhancing their sense of well-being (Fjørtoft, 2001; Muñoz, 2009; Stephenson, 2003) with positive consequences and benefits for their future learning. Fjørtoft (2001) argues that children who play regularly in an outdoor environment are less ill and physically fitter than children who do not. As distinct from playgrounds, which have become risk-free and unchallenging, the unevenness of a natural environment, such as a woodland area, offers children more of a challenge for their motoric development while demanding persistence on the part of young children to overcome obstacles. In turn, this introduces elements of risk that the children need to negotiate in order to avoid injury (Little and Eager, 2010), presenting them with the opportunity to self-appraise and self-challenge, which several empirical studies indicate is something young children desire and enjoy.

Studies in Australia (Sandseter, 2009), New Zealand (Stephenson, 2003), and Norway (Aasen et al., 2009) highlight children's exhilaration through their experience of "ambivalent" (Sandseter, 2009, p. 95) emotions during risky play, such as climbing heights or moving at speed. This, in turn, helps them to negotiate risk and develop "body mastery" (Fjørtoft, 2001, p. 117) through interacting with their environment. Stephenson (2003) considers these skills are transferrable to other areas of learning and emphasises the outdoor environment as affording children what they can't experience elsewhere. With increasing restrictions on children's activities, they currently have fewer opportunities to make their own decisions, "less opportunity to assess their own personal frontiers, and less opportunity to gain confidence and self-esteem through coping independently" (p. 42).

The links between risk-taking, physical competence, and learning are reflected in a current longitudinal study in Scotland, *Growing up in Scotland (GUS)*, involving more than 7,000 children. This study highlights a correlation between poverty and "conduct, emotional development and hyperactivity" issues (Bradshaw and Tipping, 2010, p. 13) as well as a correlation between problems with motoric development at two years and later emotional difficulties at five years old, when starting school. The latter infers body mastery (Fjørtoft, 2001), which might be linked to subsequent areas of development. This also reflects Trevarthen's (2012) suggestion that movement is closely linked to a sense of 'me,' a developing identity involving the need for self-control and self-awareness. It could be said, therefore, that children from disadvantaged areas would benefit from engaging with outdoor environments and what they have to offer.

Research in Wales (Maynard et al., 2013) and England (Murray and O'Brien, 2005) foregrounds the importance of the outdoor environment in helping build self-confidence in children from disadvantaged areas. While it could be argued that the outdoor context was a novel experience for children and teachers alike, consequently leading to changes in their behaviours, Maynard et al. (2013) conclude from their research with "underachieving children" (p. 10) that it affords the children a chance to "reconstruct (reposition) themselves as strong, competent children rather than as 'underachieving' pupils" (ibid). Although the opportunity for children's developing sense of self in the outdoor context is not yet well understood and needs more research, it could provide the backbone to a creative form of early intervention, which also nurtures children's agency. Surely this is needed for those children who are the most disadvantaged in our society.

Early intervention works

Undertaking a review of a wide range of early intervention programmes across the globe, covering 23 countries, led Nores and Barnett (2010) to state that all interventions providing education or care were effective in terms of cognitive development showing "moderate gains" (p. 272) in cognitive, behavioural, academic, and health development. Behavioural gains were significantly higher with earlier intervention including toddlers. A Scottish review of strategies led Geddes et al. (2011) to assert that early intervention helps to reduce disadvantage caused by social and environmental factors, though they suggest that using a "two generation" (p. 26) approach, incorporating support for parents, appears to create the greatest benefit. Supporting this is Siraj-Blatchford et al.'s (2011) EPPSE report (The Effective Provision of Pre-School, Primary and Secondary Education) a longitudinal study of some 3000 children aged three to sixteen years. Investigating what protective factors might be enabling some disadvantaged children to succeed where others did not, the research team defined resilience as "achievement beyond expectation" (p. i) in the face of challenge. The researchers reported that key to building self-esteem were the effects of parental support and encouragement, coupled with inspiring teachers who sought to meet the individual needs of children in their care.

Alongside the High Scope Perry Preschool project in the US, this research indicates the efficacy and prudence of early intervention. However, as Schweinhart (2013) emphasised in the original High Scope project, interventions should enable children to develop self-esteem, independent thinking, and responsibility, and the outdoor context affords children the opportunity to develop these skills and capacities. Early intervention in nature and outdoor settings can enable children to develop a sense of self through an embodied experience in an enabling environment. To extend this argument, I will now discuss the importance of movement and its relationship to children's agency.

A growing sense of 'me' and my world

Several scholars writing on consciousness, awareness, and meaning-making assert that human beings develop a sense of themselves and the world through *active engagement* with it (Damasio, 2000; McGilchrist, 2009; Merleau-Ponty, 2008; Noë, 2004; Trevarthen, 2012; Tuan, 1977; Varela, 1999). Both Varela (1999, p. 13) and Noë (2004, p. 227) use the term "enactive approach" to describe the need for experience through the senses and therefore the body to make meaning of the world. Perception is "intrinsically active," writes Noë (p. 3), and requires "sensorimotor bodily skill" to perceive it (p. 11). His notion of embodiment is coupled with a developing sense of self through experiences that are ever-changing and in turn inform each individual's world. Tuan (1977) concurs, stating that the sense of self develops through the exercise of power and agency.

An emphasis on movement and its role in constructing individual worlds, "perceiver-dependent" worlds as opposed to "pre-given" (Varela, 1999, p. 13) worlds, is highlighted by Varela:

> Cognitive science is waking up to the full importance of the realization that perception does not consist in the recovery of a pre-given world, but rather in the perceptual guidance of action in a world that is inseparable from our sensorimotor capacities, and that "higher" cognitive structures also emerge from recurrent patterns of perceptually guided action. Thus cognition consists not of representations but of *embodied action*. Thus we can say that the world we know is not pre-given; it is, rather *enacted...*
>
> *(p. 17)*

Active learning, movement, and the development of a sense of self is familiar to early years practitioners through the work of Piaget (1971). More recently Trevarthen (2012) emphasised the vital importance of the sense of self-movement (proprioceptive sense) in helping children to feel "alive" (p. 306) as they learn to control their bodies and become self-aware. He suggests that children are "by nature imaginative, concerned and sociable, eager to claim a place in the world of meaning and responsibility, and to be able to tell stories about it" (p. 307); children come to know their world through exploration. Trevarthen's insightful research involving babies and young toddlers indicates that, on the whole, children strive to be included, to be sociable and to explore, to develop their sense of self.

Building on the work of several phenomenologists, McGilchrist (2009) expresses the role of resistance in awakening awareness by stating: "I come into being as a self through the experience of resistance, as a lake is bounded by the shore which makes it a lake" (p. 224). This suggests that when something new is encountered, there is the chance to evaluate what is known with what is newly encountered and subsequently to evolve knowledge to a new level. Resistance is therefore a catalyst in coming to know the world and self. Young children would, therefore, benefit from the possibility of encountering resistance through the use of their senses, which in the natural landscape is heightened as nothing remains the same; the weather changes, vegetation grows and decays, the clouds move and alter, the animals and insects are varied throughout the year, flowers colour the landscape then disappear, soil turns to mud in the rain, birds migrate; everything changes constantly, stimulating the senses. Further significance is given to this by Gibson's (1986) assertion, noted previously, that children perceive the environment holistically but note any change that takes place, any variable consequently impacting on their sensing and knowing. However, there are many challenges and impediments to working with young children outdoors, not least of which is risk, a factor that impacts on practitioners' desire to be outdoors with their children. This is amplified through society's culture of fear, noted previously by Furedi (2006) in which 'good' parenting may be defined as protecting children from harm rather than chancing possible injury through outdoor play.

A risky affair

As a consequence of parental fears, children today are growing up "without the enabling risks and challenges," often conferred through outdoor play (Hope et al., 2007, p. 328). Yet, the avoidance of risk and injury makes play spaces boring and "challenge free" (Stephenson, 2003, p. 40), which in turn leads young children to actively seek out challenge and stimulation elsewhere. Asserting that fear is what currently shapes the "cultural imagination of the early twenty-first century," Furedi (2006, p. vii) suggests children remain under constant adult surveillance, unable to take risks, having been taught that "the outside world is a no-go area" (p. xix). This culture, predicated on anxiety and fear, legitimises safety as a virtue and, consequently, taking risks as "irresponsible behaviour" (p. 9). Early years education and care, however, has a long-standing history of valuing the importance of the outdoor context (Blanchet-Cohen and Elliot, 2011) and as all of the previously mentioned research suggests, it can provide all children, but especially those from disadvantaged backgrounds, with a context in which to flourish. Such a dilemma leaves those practitioners willing to take children outdoors, at risk themselves of being accused of being irresponsible risk-takers. With the publication of '*My World Outdoors*' by the Care Inspectorate (2016) in Scotland, practitioners are being actively encouraged to use the outdoor context as part of daily practice in early years settings, to offset obesity, increase wellbeing and make links to their local environment. For many practitioners, however, the risks involved may still be seen as a step too far and, despite extra training in outdoor practices coupled with the assurance and legitimation of such practices by the Care Inspectorate's document, only time will tell if practitioners feel safe enough to take risks.

The early intervention work I engaged with (see Chapter 2 and Chapter 3) was intuitively based at the time – albeit consequent to my having worked with children over a long period of time, building a sense for what worked. It was later developed further through becoming acquainted with research, enabling me to appreciate more fully the possibility for children to develop a new sense of themselves. Although I am mindful of Whitty's (2001) caution that we need to avoid "naïve possibilitarianism" (p. 288) and McMillan's caution from 1912 that "Nothing evens up this gross injustice" of poverty (cited in Reay, 2001, p. 333), I concur wholeheartedly with Smyth and McInerney (2013), who state that it is not optional to take a "disinterested stance" in the face of injustice (p. 15). Action is needed now and I for one would advocate more outdoor play and experiences for the youngest members of our society. Darren helped me to experience this and so I continue to argue its case.

Postscript: Darren's tree

A few years ago, I visited a close ex-colleague and friend. After a while, we chatted about the children we both knew from our early years work.

SARA: Do you remember Darren?

EH: How could I forget him? He was simply adorable, cheeky and so full of life.

SARA: He did well in high school, you'll be glad to know, and works for the council as a pool attendant at the swimming pool in town. He has a wee baby too and lives with his partner near the new supermarket. But did you hear about his wee cousin Jamie?

EH: No, I didn't. What's up?

SARA: You didn't hear it on the news then? Last year?

EH: What news last year? You forget I'm hundreds of miles away now!

Sara pauses for a moment, looks away then glances back. I begin to feel uneasy.

SARA: Well, late one night after Jamie and his mates had been playing up at the old rubbish dump near the canal, they decided to walk home past the allotment site. They were a bit high and it was cold, so they decided to break into the sheds to keep warm. After finding some sticks, matches, a can of petrol, paper, and a few seats, they decided to start a bonfire. I don't really know what happened but somehow or other Jamie caught light. The other kids panicked and ... and ... well, they ran away. (She pauses and struggles to carry on.) A driver passing by saw the flames and Jamie running through the allotments. He called for an ambulance and took a travel-blanket from his car to smother the flames, but he was too late. By the time the ambulance arrived, Jamie had died.

EH: Oh my God! ... No, no, no, no, no! (I grasp her arm.) Stop! Don't speak! I can't cope with this!

I try to stifle my pain but don't manage and emit a strange, deep, primal sound. My body convulses. Sara turns away as tears roll down her face. Then we stand apart in silence.

The river flows gently by and the cows in the nearby field phlegmatically moo. A few gulls squawk overhead as a storm builds up in the air. There is a slight breeze and it moves my hair slowly across my face and over my closed eyes.

We remain still and quiet for a while before Sara moves, beckoning me to follow. She stops near a big tree. I know this tree ... this is Darren's tree, the one he hugged many years ago. It's a tree that often attracted little children's attention. It was so wide it needed several children to link arms to encircle it and its uppermost branches seemed to go on for ever, right through the clouds. Sara places her hand on the tree and strokes it, as though she's caressing a baby, then turns to me and speaks.

SARA: When Jamie came here on his first day he ran straight up to this tree and looking up, said "This is my tree" then he hugged it. This is it. This is all that's left now. I miss him. I miss Jamie.

4

LISTENING TO LOLA

Embodying care and safeguarding

'Somebody' haiku (i)
all year she has wondered
why folk imagine she is
somebody else

(Thewless, 2009)

Lola has decided she wants to play with the small-world toys today: wooden houses, furniture, and people built on a small scale to resemble real life. I don't much like them myself: one tall, wooden, two-storey house divided into four flats, peopled with wooden characters and furniture that I inherited when I arrived in the nursery, and one wooden 'cottage-style' house with flowers painted on the front. These toys leave little to the imagination and I had thought that I might put them in the cupboard for a while.

Lola plays alone, talking to herself, and I shuffle books around on the shelf while keeping an eye on her and eavesdropping. She often lashes out at other kids and it quickly turns nasty, so I'm a bit wary when Mark creeps slowly towards Lola's territory. Lola has already placed the wooden 'dad' doll in the kitchen with the wooden 'mum.' Using the wooden 'girl' doll to represent herself, she places it on the table with an imaginary toy. Taking another child-like doll, she calls it Mikey (her brother) and sits it on the sofa before placing a doll to represent Frankie (her oldest sibling) in the corner of the room with an imaginary Xbox. Summer, Lola's baby sister, is the baby-doll in the cot. Suddenly, 'dad' comes out of the kitchen and with one fast hand-move, sweeps 'Lola' violently the length of the table then onto the floor, while shouting "You little rat, I'll get you! I've told you not to sit on that table!" She repeats this twice.

I nod to my colleague. She nods back. Mark moves away, quietly sensing danger.

> Since 2008 more children on the Child Protection Register are under 5 years old than over. In 2014, 53% of children on the register were under 5 years. Between 2000 and 2014 the overall increase in numbers of children on the register rose by 41%.
>
> *(Scottish Government, 2015, np)*

After a pause, Lola takes her family characters and gets them ready to go to the corner shop. Frankie asks to stay behind with his Xbox, so the others leave the house without him. Suddenly the Lola doll and the Mikey doll begin to squabble and fight, so Ricky shouts at them both. Then, as they pass the refuse-bin cupboards at the bottom of the flats (Lola has placed a plastic pirate's treasure chest beside the wooden play house), Ricky opens the door and puts a black bag full of rubbish into the bin, then, swiftly turning round, grabs Lola and throws her inside, shouting, "Get in there, you little rat, and shut it 'til we get back!" He turns the key and walks on. Lola takes the other dolls and walks them to the corner shop. She is engrossed in thought, and I wonder if she knows I'm watching and listening.

My stomach muscles tighten and my hands instantly freeze. I quickly turn and nod to one of my colleagues. She nods back, signalling she has heard it too. Then, quietly, I move towards Lola's play space. We're in Child Protection/ Safeguarding territory now and I fear where this is going. My stomach turns over, my hands tremble, my breath becomes shallow, but this is no time to turn away. I need to engage sensitively and quietly as the room is crowded with other children playing and running around. Anything might happen.

Taking a wooden 'grandma' doll, I walk behind Lola's family to the 'shop.' "Hello," I say to them all. "Are you off shopping?" We've built up enough trust now for Lola to allow me into her play-world, but it's erratic and I know that time is precious; she might just let me in for a few seconds, so I have to act fast. But she doesn't reply. Is she ignoring me? Did she hear me? I don't know. Breathe deeply. Think of something appropriate to say...

"Buying anything nice, today?" I enquire brightly. Pause.

"No... just bread and milk." Her voice sounds wistful and far away.

"Did Lola not want to come to the shops?" I ask. Pause.

She throws the wooden daddy doll into the air, thumping it with her fist when it lands. She takes the other wooden dolls and scatters them across the floor then, in silence, walks away to the other side of the nursery. I look at my colleague and we nod to one another. I tremble with fear. I think Sandra, my colleague, senses it too. I start to squeeze my cold, icy fingers, gripped by the solitude and tension I'm feeling. The responsibility is overwhelming and I sense a numbing cold travelling up my arms. I feel unable to speak and the thought of having to interact with Ricky fills me with dread.

As I move away, to discreetly record the event before I forget any details, I feel my stomach twist as though it's in a wrench. My pulse races and I have to gasp for extra air as a nauseous feeling wells up and tightens my throat. I hate having to deal with Child Protection and Safeguarding cases. I hate it, hate it. It sends a chill air into my body.

I quickly stagger to the toilet as I start to gag. The loneliness of the responsibility fills me with dark dread as the duty falls on me to inform. Suddenly an unexpected feeling rises up. I struggle to understand it. I'm perplexed. As I slowly breathe out, however, I come to recognise just how much I fear and despise Ricky. In fact, I've come to loathe him and can't face the thought of having to interact with him. Will he leave me alone now or will this make things worse? Then I quickly do a double-take, a rain-check on my soul. I feel sick and start to wretch as I mutter, "Oh, my God! What have I become?"

In the toilet, I sink to the floor, overcome with fear and self-disgust. My body slides limply down the wall, before coming to rest in a doubled-up position on my knees, my head resting on the floor between the wall and the toilet bowl. I sob quietly and tremble with the overwhelming emotions; caught between two worlds – the self I thought I was and the self that just came into view – I am still and cold, enveloped in the silence that permeates no-man's land, on the toilet floor. "What is this being human all about?" I ask myself. "What is it that pushes us into such dark places where our light is all but snuffed out?"

The sounds of the nursery slowly begin to drift in under the door: laughter, children calling to each other, wooden blocks tumbling to the floor, the soft tones of the practitioners talking to each other, the phone ringing in the background, the sound of water being poured in and out of a container. Leaning on the toilet bowl, I draw myself up into a standing position before dragging my heavy, aching body over to the wash-hand basin to throw cold water on my face. Catching sight of a pale, grey face in the mirror, I ask, "Is this me? Who am I?" Then I turn to the door and slowly, tentatively, unlock it, before re-entering the world.

★ ★ ★

Embodied knots: Caring, fear, and power

Dealing with Child Protection incidents was never a routine matter for me, thankfully, but no matter how often I dealt with them, I always felt ill afterwards, vomiting and crying. Maybe it's the same for other practitioners? I'm not sure why it had such an impact on me, but I suspect that it had something to do with my reluctance to associate myself with the power of such judgements and the consequences for families. After all, aren't we all flawed? And the circumstances of some people's lives, far worse than mine, might be something

I also could not endure. However, I firmly uphold the imperative to protect children from harm, which creates a moral and emotional dilemma within my professional practice. I feel stuck in the middle, in an emotional no-man's land. What should we do with the feelings that arise in moments like these? With little time to think, let alone seek counsel and help for disturbing anxieties, expressing such thoughts and feelings at work might be interpreted as a sign of weakness, as someone unfit for purpose. Yet, these feelings simply do not disappear: They linger like a soul-mist, reappearing at unexpected moments throughout a lifetime.

The situation with Ricky and Lola was very unusual and complex, however, because I'd never had to deal with a parent who had such intimate knowledge of my family and that terrified me. As it turned out, social services talked to Ricky and his girlfriend and dealt with some of the issues causing trauma and angst at home. But when they discussed the possible outcomes of the refuse-bin cupboard incident with Ricky, he broke down and sobbed after confessing to throwing Lola in and locking the door. After much discussion and debate, he and the social workers agreed that he needed support and several strategies were consequently put in place, including attending parenting classes at school. He was also given a helpline number to call when he was not coping so that nothing untoward would happen again and he agreed to ease up on his drinking.

For my part, I carried on struggling with Child Protection responsibilities and never quite got over the scare with Ricky. Although I genuinely admired and applauded Ricky's efforts to change his life with Gemma, eventually attending college to train as a builder, he left an incisive mark on me and the re-telling of this story here, now, brought it all home again. At the time of our interaction, I drew on my creativity, my belief in human beings, my supportive colleagues, family, and friends, to try to get over it. But, if I'm honest, it still hurts and I still feel the fear. Such was the shock.

This story encapsulates the profound impact of emotional tension within early years work (and other front-line services) and its consequences: the embodied knot wrought with pain and fear. It raises the possibility that a part of me did not fully move through the knot, instead becoming deeply entangled in it, lost even, for a while.

Describing the way in which a tree creates a whorl around new growth, such as a branch as it tries to emerge from the old bark, Ingold (2015) suggests that as the tree continues to grow, the knot becomes more dense, "compressed into a hard core" (p. 19). Another type of knot, he states, a pre-formed knot, exists within the human body. This knot, a tube-like form manifesting in a knotted shape, draws in the spent blood before sending it out again as oxygenated blood, a life-giving force: It is the heart. Perhaps it is between these two – the whorl and the heart – the story of Ricky and Lola resides for it is still palpable, today, as I sit and write.

Among other things, this story challenges the myth that both caring and emotional work are simply natural traits of early years workers, raising the issue of a need to further understand the complexity of emotional intelligence and emotional labour. How might we work with them in the early years' context and how might we nurture practitioner well-being?

Unravelling the knots: caring and emotion

Beyond caring?

In the last decade or so, a number of writers have highlighted the growing pressure on early years workers through increased government attention and regulation (Ball, 2003,2015a, 2015b; Hargreaves, 2000; Jensen, 2014; Jensen et al., 2010; Lazzari, 2014; Moyles, 2001; Osgood, 2012). Heightened global competition, in turn, catalysed the creation of regimes of accountability as early education was hailed as the saviour of future economic success of the nation (Jensen, 2014; Lazzari, 2014; Osgood, 2012). Identifying early education and childcare (ECEC) as the context with the most significant impact on children's learning, the European Commission in its turn encouraged promotion of the sector to achieve "sustainable growth" (Lazzari, 2014, p. 427). Such changes have impacted the workforce and their identity leading Ball (2003) to state that teachers are struggling in very personal ways, affecting their "belief and commitment, service and even love, and ... mental health and emotional well-being" (p. 216). He emphasised "This is the struggle over the teachers' soul" (p. 217).

Growing regimes of accountability have increased tension between two distinctly different early years discourses namely those based on social investment paradigms and those based on children's rights (Basford and Bath, 2014; Lazzari, 2014). Moyles (2001, p. 82) has described the dissonance as challenging and threatening teachers' "passion" within the profession, while Basford and Bath (2014) argue such tensions force practitioners to simply play the game. Hargreaves (2000), however, notes a "disturbing neglect of the emotional dimension in the increasingly rationalized world of educational reform" (p. 811). What these tensions foreground is the lack of a theoretical and practical approach within early years work that balances and unites care and education, leading to significant controversy and tension within the profession. Consequently, the move to an outcomes-led culture has meant those activities that were measurable became highly visible while caring, perceived as more ephemeral and less tangible, became "invisible" (Forrester, 2005, p. 271) and devalued. The roots of these tensions, however, are embedded within historical perspectives of women and their perceived 'natural' ability to care. These are explored in the section that follows.

Room for care?

The similarities that can be drawn between early years work and mothering, especially the importance of children's physical well-being and the concomitant physical tasks, historically led to the conflation of these two roles within early years work and a consequent genderization of the workforce (Osgood, 2012). Caring and "nurturing" were seen as "instinctive female attribute(s)" (Forrester, 2005, p. 273) and, consequently, little real discourse on the matter of caring and the level of emotional commitment involved in early years work took place. The meaning of the word 'educate' derives from the Latin word '*educare*' meaning 'to rear,' which suggests notions of "intimacy and nurturance" (Gitlin and Myers, 1993, p. 66), a concept historically associated with women. However, a devaluing of nurturing and a tension between policy and practice developed as schools, agencies of "control and compliance," stood in opposition to the more "gender-related" (ibid) terms, intimating closeness and nurturing.

The need to legitimise education through "scientific approaches" (Goldstein, 1998, p. 259) after the First World War relegated the "softer and more humanistic aspects" of early years work to the margins and "eclipsed the central importance of caring" (ibid). Consequently, the importance of the affective skills needed by practitioners to further develop children's social and emotional well-being was underplayed, relegating these matters to personal concern or as Lewis (1993, p. 5) has it "personal burdens." As Hargreaves (2000, p. 813) states:

> Being tactful, caring or compassionate as a teacher is treated as largely a matter of personal disposition, moral commitment or private virtue, rather than of how particular ways of organizing teaching shape teachers' emotional experiences.

The continued tensions created as a result of this are, I believe, responsible for much of the stress reported by researchers from a wide variety of empirical studies, which highlight a lack of understanding of the demands and consequences of emotional labour (Forrester, 2005; Osgood, 2012; Page and Elfer, 2013). They also contribute to the rise in "burnout" (Forrester, 2005, p. 284) and workforce attrition through "friction between teachers' performing and caring activities" (ibid) as illustrated in several of my stories. Kyriacou (1987) has described burnout as "the syndrome resulting from prolonged teacher stress" (p. 146), a key component of which is emotional exhaustion. Løvgren (2016), in her recent study of 2,500 childcare workers in Norway, noted a correlation between emotional exhaustion and "teaching- and parent-oriented tasks" (p. 165) among the managers and teachers in her study, who are also recognised as perceiving above-average stress in the workplace (Schreyer and Krause, 2016). Emotional exhaustion is one of several factors recognised as contributing to burnout; others involve a sense of loss of control or depersonalization, a feeling of limited personal accomplishment and a sense of not being valued (Ball, 2010; Rentzou, 2012; Løvgren, 2016).

While some of these factors are consequent to situational tensions and the effect of policy implementation, what Løvgren noted may be an illustration of the tension between two very different aspects of early years work, teaching and caring, coupled with the regular, daily contact with parents. The failure to resolve tensions and to maintain a sense of coherence in practitioners' personal narratives is seen as a contributing factor in the choice of many to leave the profession by Downey et al. (2014). Yet, most research on attrition previously erased the lives of teachers (Schaefer et al., 2014), suggesting to me a further reason for the inclusion of self-reflexive narratives in research, raising the visibility of key tensions experienced by practitioners.

Caring is an intrinsic part of early years work and current empirical research on practitioner identity notes that words used to describe their practice, such as caring/empathic/compassionate, highlight a strong commitment to "empathic approaches" (Osgood, 2012, p. 78) and a deep connection to the "affective domain" (p. 132). A counter-narrative, however, was also revealed in the same research as some practitioners noted the need for "detachment" and "demarcation of private from professional self" (p. 132) in their work. Perhaps these findings identify a key factor within the debate on teacher attrition, namely the juggling of tensions within the early years field, a matter also evident in my stories?

I believe there are three key strands to understanding the tensions around caring in early years work. I want to explore these as a way of unravelling the knot around caring and emotional work in early years practice as it features largely in my stories: (i) the conflation of mothering and early years work which naturalises caring, (ii) the impact of the context of early years settings and (iii) the lack of understanding of emotional input/demand.

Caring knots 1: woman-care to embodiment

Drawing attention to women's ways of expressing themselves Gilligan (1982, 1993) helped catalyse an overdue discourse on women's voices. Her intention to change the "voice of the world" through the incorporation of women's voices was based on her feminist stance in which she emphasised the "courage and emotional stamina" (1993, p. xix) of women in relationships, which was undervalued and merited attention. Writing at around the same time, Noddings (2003, 1984) drew attention to women's work in caring, promoting their role through the notion that women were "better equipped for caring than men are" (p. 97). Noddings considered caring was pivotal to the self-image of many women, though she acknowledged that biological, psychological, and socializing factors were possibly all at work. Linking caring to mothering in acts of "engrossment" (Noddings, 1988, p. 220) in which the carer identified completely and was perfectly attuned to the one being cared-for, Noddings emphasised relationality in an *ethic of care*. She distinguished between the feeling of duty in caring ('I must') and the drive or choice to want to care ('I ought/want') to improve a situation, the latter as "moral imperative" (Noddings, 2003, 1984, p. 82). However, presenting the skills necessary and relevant for teaching as natural attributes of women, as "maternal thinking" and "caring," (Noddings, 1988, p. 220) Noddings created an obstacle to recognising the "emotional costs" of caring (Isenbarger and Zembylas, 2006, p. 123).

In Goldstein's words, this "traps women in an oppressive, stereotyped, and tradition-bound set of roles and behaviours," thereby perpetuating "inequalities and subjugations" (1998, p. 247). Moving beyond the view of caring as natural and simply about "gentle smiles and warm hugs" (p. 259), Goldstein utilised Noddings' 'ethic of care' but took a feminist moral stance to help increase awareness of the intellectual challenge involved in working with children and its complexity. Drawing the distinction between a feminine and a feminist ethic of care, Gilligan (1995) asserts that a feminist ethic of care problematises the silenced and assumptive notions bound to a feminine ethic of care that assumes selflessness and self-sacrifice on the part of women to care. A feminist perspective challenges the "patriarchal social order" within which this notion has developed and reframes caring within a "discourse of relationship" (p. 122) to become a voice of "resistance" (p. 123).

Currently the concept of embodiment within care and education has become visible through the work of "third-wave feminist" theorists (van Laere et al., 2014, p. 239) who have moved the debate beyond earlier feminist research. Early feminist research focussed attention on social constructions of women and, later, women's rights and those of other marginalised groups that challenged patriarchal power structures. Currently, the drive in feminist research encompasses embodiment, which goes beyond the bounds of gender and the mind-body dualism in western discourse and practices that have, historically, given preference to issues of the mind over the body, privileging cognition over the practical intelligences embedded in the body. The concept of embodiment incorporates the role of the senses and emotions, their connection to space and place, and their impact on human beings; the core site of embodied experiences is the body (Bartos, 2013).

It is important to consider embodiment within early years work further as the extensive time adults and children spend together and the intensity of their relationships distinguish the practice from other forms of work where relationships are more temporal (van Laere et al., 2014). It follows then that a denial of "embodied subjectivity" (p. 240) also denies emotion, "feelings, passion or pleasure" (ibid), which in my experience are part of daily nursery life. As van Laere et al. (2014) clearly state:

> Care, referring to love, tactility and bodily emissions, takes us back to forgotten issues of children who are being and becoming citizens, and enables us to draw on a diversity of embodied experiences of both men and women in the ECEC workforce.
>
> *(p. 239)*

The importance of warm, caring relationships in early childhood cannot be underestimated and many writers emphasise the seriousness of the consequences of a deficit. Layard and Dunn (2009, p. 173) contest it leads to an "emotional narrowing, an empathy deficit" that leads to later life challenges. This is illustrated incisively in the trial of an American mass murderer in which the judge concluded that a key contributing factor to his extreme behaviour lay in a childhood lacking in warmth; instead, it had been filled with "abuse and play-lessness" (Sheets-Johnstone, 2003, p. 409).

Loving relationships in infancy and the need for attuned, sensitive adults, able to be responsive to children's needs, to be "emotionally available," is particularly important for children separated from their primary carers in care contexts (Gerhardt, 2004, p. 74). Gerhardt, in her work on love, makes a clear and compelling case for early positive attachments and bonds in relationships, to provide infants with a context in which they can learn emotional control and well-being. At variance with this position are Dahlberg et al. (2007), who assert that "closeness and intimacy" are "problematic" (p. 82). They view practitioners in early years settings as researchers and colleagues in children's learning experiences. Their stance, based on children's agency, has its place in helping to remind practitioners that children are not weak and vulnerable; they can also be seen as empowered and strong. However, there is a substantial body of work to suggest that close, responsive relationships nurture attachment and a sense of belonging and well-being, setting the foundation for emotional well-being and later learning. Current writing on the affective dimensions of pedagogy suggests affect underpins both cognition and behaviour, yet it is still little understood (Watkins, 2010).

Several of the children I worked with in my career grew up in challenging circumstances in which their parents struggled with "unmanageable internal pain" (Gerhardt, 2004, p. 153) and "few inner resources" (p. 151), which led to barriers between themselves and their children. Consequently the children often expressed avoidant behaviours as they had not learned how to cope within the safety of secure, stable relationships. Gerhardt's emphasis on the links between early experiences deprived of attention, love, and closeness is a stark warning to all those involved in early years work: practitioners, policy-makers, and managers alike. Not to include warmth and closeness allows a "vicious circle" (p. 148) to perpetuate that I feel is morally and socially unacceptable.

Embodiment is one way to explore the impact of all of the above on practitioners because as a concept, it also highlights the complex nature of emotion. However, embodiment as an emotional geography is under-researched in education (Kenway and Youdell, 2011), despite its relevance to early years work. What follows therefore focuses on emotional geographies and explores the impact of emotion on practitioners.

Caring knots 2: embodied places?

While many practitioners associate their work with caring (Forrester, 2005; Hargreaves, 2000; Isenbarger and Zembylas, 2006; Vogt, 2002; Watkins, 2011), such intimacy between practitioners, children, and their families both forges deep bonds *and* heightens the intensity of relationships within early years settings. Several scholars have indicated that this is a key component *of* and tension *within* early years work (Elfer and Dearnley, 2007; Hargreaves, 2000; Moyles, 2001) and recognise its role in creating an "affectively charged" (Watkins, 2011, p. 138) context that differentiates early years from other educational settings such as high school or college.

Illustrating such a difference is one study by Hargreaves (2000) of fifty-three teachers in both primary and high schools, which led him to conclude that high school teachers view emotion as getting in the way of work and therefore in need of neutralization, but early primary settings were deemed to be places of "emotional intensity" (p. 824). Professionals in the early primary settings were expected to nurture interactions that supported emotional well-being through close relationships, imbued with warmth, within contexts that were perceived to be caring places. Extending this to early years settings, it is easy to see that emotional intensity is further heightened by spatial considerations, as adults and children are usually located within the same room/area for the whole year, leading to deep associations and embodiment of spatial location. Deep bonds and interactions within these contexts therefore create an embodied affect that does not "simply dissipate" (Watkins, 2011, p. 140) but resides in the body. Perhaps this is in part due to the limited time in which to stand back and consider relationships in any significant and professional way in daily practice.

As a space gains meaning and definition, it becomes a place, a more intimate area. For children, this involves coming to know a place through their senses in a deeper way than is usual for adults. Place then becomes "a pause in movement" (Tuan, 1977, p. 138) a place to simply be, to be present. Humanist geographers have drawn on the work of the phenomenologist Merleau-Ponty (1962) in their attempts to understand place and its relationship to people through his concept of being-in-the-world. Bartos (2013) suggests that the body is the primary place in which we encounter the world and is therefore the seat of a "felt geography" (p. 90) characterised by emotional experiences over prolonged time.

Embodied lives

During Watkins' (2011) empirical research with five teachers that focussed on their practice, she noted that they often shed tears when recalling their work. She suggested this relates to

> an embodiment of each teacher's specific investment or interest in teaching which had accumulated through the process of the pedagogic exchange enacted in schools and classrooms as teachers practiced their craft... This suggests something profound about the ethical dimension of teaching... at the intersection of bodies and space, through which we come to be.
>
> *(p. 142)*

The exchange Watkins refers to relates to teachers' desire both to care for and love the children in their care as well as their own desire for reciprocity. Watkins suggests this in turn underpins both the "desire to learn and the desire to teach" (2010, p. 271). The interiorising of these experiences, an embodiment of experience garnered through interactions with children, subsequently proves "formative in shaping subjectivity" (ibid), transforming those engaged in the reciprocal relationships (Zembylas, 2004).

My story-writing "re:membered" (Brogden, 2008, p. 855) my work with young children, deeply imbued with my intention to care, my concerns over their welfare and well-being, their safety, and health and happiness. Yet this work was simultaneously situated at the conflicting boundaries of state intervention through child protection/safeguarding, regulatory demands for outcomes and targets, and parental expectation leading to professional and personal tensions. The unravelling of my personal investment in my career, predicated on my intention to love and care for young children, was a challenging experience when writing. I then began to consider whether most of the stories I was writing illustrated moments that had demanded more intense engagement with the children in my care, linked to the possibility of not succeeding in my task. These "turning-point" events (Denzin, 2014a, p. x) had caused extreme discomfort, rupturing my identity, which may have consequently created an embodiment of dissonant emotion. Riessman (2008, p. 10) writes "When biographical disruptions occur that rupture expectations for continuity, individuals make sense of these events through storytelling." Was I engaged in a process of self-healing as well as meaning-making?

In struggling to help children to be, not just to know, do we as practitioners journey into an ontological realm that demands greater engagement and therefore deeper emotional investment? If, as Watkins (2011, p. 138) suggests, early years settings are highly "affectively charged" contexts, the question remains as to why there is still little consideration given to the emotional investment demanded of professionals? These unanswered questions need further research, especially as nurturing approaches with young children have, rightly in my view, gained currency within educational practices in Scotland. With the publication of documentation from Education Scotland and Glasgow City Council (2017), advocating for whole school nurturing approaches, practitioners are now being expected to care more for the children in their care, but just what does that mean and cost, especially in areas of multiple deprivation?

Caring knots 3: caring exchanges

With the introduction of the term "emotional labour" (Hochschild, 2012, p. 7), expression was given to a form of work that necessitated masking true emotion in favour of a performed emotion within the workplace, constituting the "management of feeling" (ibid). Drawing on the work of Hochschild led Isenbarger and Zembylas (2006) to caution against ignoring real feelings felt by practitioners in education as it may lead to "burnout" (p. 122) of teachers who are committed to their role in helping transform children's lives. Foregrounding the importance of recognising "felt emotions" (p. 133), Isenbarger and Zembylas indicate that emotional labour forces teachers to hide or mask their true feelings when dealing with children. They consider the amount of emotional labour involved in work with young children is underestimated, as is the need for practitioners to be resourceful and resilient emotionally, yet this is a neglected area of research. Hargreaves (2000, p. 811) concurs, asserting a "disturbing neglect of the emotional dimension in the increasingly rationalized world of educational reform."

Although there is a growing body of research that asserts the need for emotional work in early years practice, there is the danger that it is solely associated with the work of women (King, 1998). Vogt's (2002) research in both Swiss and English primary schools demonstrates this is not the whole picture.

Men caring

Vogt's (2002) empirical research adds an important voice to the debate on emotion and caring in early years work and the need to include emotion and caring in the early research agenda. Her empirical study with 32 English and Swiss primary teachers, male and female, focused on caring within teaching. She noted women constitute 88% of the primary teaching workforce in England and Wales compared to 73% in Switzerland. Her findings suggested that both men and women share the view that an ethic of care is important in teaching, that they employ it equally and similarly place relationships at the heart of their view of themselves as teachers. The teachers' conceptions of caring, spread across a spectrum, included caring as commitment, relatedness, physical care, giving a cuddle, parenting, and mothering (p. 257). Vogt concluded that the concept of caring "does not depend on the teacher's gender" (p. 262) and went on to assert that we should not "perpetuate the discourse of feminism and gender difference" (p. 262) with respect to caring.

Vogt's findings are important to include here for although there is broad agreement from many researchers that emotional engagement and sensitivity are essential to early years work it should not be seen as an exclusively feminine issue. A further study of two primary teachers, one male and one female, carried out in the UK by Goouch (2010), explored intuitive practices in education which she defined as the ability to "respect the intentionality of children" and to respond intuitively and sensitively using children's "created narratives" (p. 42). Goouch's research led her to indicate that both teachers recognised the importance of "encounter" (p. 133) and reflexivity, illustrating their ability to care. However, it must be recognised that she also chose these two teachers because of their sensitive working practices.

A tentative conclusion that caring in education is not gender-specific can be drawn from these studies, bearing in mind small sample sizes. The dearth of research into the caring practices of early years workers and women in particular is, I believe, part of the wider research issue that neglected the body, emotion, and sensory experience noted earlier in this book and that autoethnography seeks to address.

While I acknowledge the need for research and understanding on emotions, I feel that the tensions and challenges for practitioners go beyond performed emotions to factors that are out of their control, yet, significantly impact on their well-being, as I will now argue.

Can you feel me?

A mark of good early years practice often cites the importance of observations, sensitive attunement to children's needs, and sustained shared attention/thinking (Goldstein, 1999; Goouch, 2010; Nutbrown, 2006). This practice demands awareness and wakefulness on the part of the practitioner to what is going on around them and infers that practitioners need emotional intelligence. Goleman (1996), who popularised emotional intelligence, however, presented it in very individualistic terms, such as how an individual might relate to others' emotional states or perceive their own emotional signals. Yet, as Hargreaves (2000) indicates, emotions are not simply situated within our minds, they are relational, "embedded and expressed in human interactions and relationships" (p. 824). In other words, they are dynamic and meaningfully situated within reciprocal relationships with others and they are embodied. Attunement and sensitive observations also call on practitioners to open up their senses, to see the problem as if "through the child's eyes" (Goldstein, 1999, p. 661), intensifying the embodied experience.

What is often overlooked here, however, is the impact of these activities on the embodied experiences of practitioners as they try to see the world through the eyes of their children and to sense their needs, feel them, hear them, and to share in moments of wonder and awe. The research lens is usually focused on the child's experience, but I assert the impact on the practitioner also needs consideration within the context of embodied experience and its consequences, as I will now discuss.

Current literature in neuroscience has had a considerable impact on education, but as Trevarthen (2012, p. 304) cautions, it can be a "reductive doctrine" when applied to children and education. Yet, it also allows useful insight such as that described below and is therefore, I believe, worthy of attention at this point.

Engaging deeply through shared attention or sensitive observations requires practitioners to be open. Currently, neurologists assert that we respond neurologically to events in which we are participating through the functioning of mirror neurons that link visual perceptions to the "proprioceptive sense of one's own capabilities" (Gallagher, 2005, p. 77). In other words, when we see something, we respond inwardly as though engaging in the same activity, even when we are observers. Mirror neurons, as Gallagher (2005) indicates, are used both in action *and* when observing action. They activate the "relevant brain areas that correspond(s) to my perception of that action" (p. 222), enabling an observer to "read(s) off the meaning of the other" (ibid) from within and are considered crucial to children's imitative actions. Neuroscientists debate whether this action is simulated within or immediately experienced as a first-person action, but either way, there is an internalised experience of what is happening externally. As Gallagher states:

> … mirror neurons or shared representations respond *both* when a particular motor action is performed by the subject *and* when the subject observes the same goal-directed action performed by another individual.
>
> *(p. 220)*

Although the relevance of mirror neurons is situated within motoric actions and not emotional experiences, their relevance within embodiment becomes clearer when linked to Ahmed's (2004, p. 185) notion that fear contracts the body, such as "in anticipation of injury." This suggests to me that practitioners, engaged in close, sensitive work with young children, are subject to a constant stream of inner experiences within the body at a level below conscious registration. If these experiences are traumatic and emotionally demanding, they may lead to the interiorisation of children's fears and bodily contractions within complex and demanding contexts. Conversely, Ahmed recognises that wonder expands the body: "Wonder keeps bodies and space open to the surprise of others" (p. 183).

My stories in Part I of this book are deeply inflected with troubling, unresolved issues that I still carry. I am marked by them and wonder to what extent working within challenging contexts, filled with tensions, led to a deep embodiment of emotional experiences. As Palmer (2007) has it, our work involves practices of the heart, borne out of the practice of allowing ourselves on a daily basis to be vulnerable, but I suggest this comes at a price to the practitioner.

PART II

Your world, my world, our embodied world

5

LIGHT AND SOUND

Negotiating illness and the final threshold

she introduces
her baby to his shadow:
he waves, it waves back

(Jenkins, 2011, p. 15)

He walks slowly around the room with hands outstretched, searching. I watch
him for several minutes before realising that he's chasing sunbeams. As he finds
each one, he sensuously runs his hands over the object it touches: first the wall,
then the room divider, the door, the floor. He makes a humming sound, a deep
ocean-like sound, and I can see from his body he is delighting in his finds. He
rolls his body across the wall and laughs. He rolls it back again and then looks
to see if the sunbeam is still there. It is and it's sparkling and more radiant now
as the clouds have gone and the sun is in full glory in the sky. He wipes the wall
with his face, his cheeks to be more exact, and then with his eyes only a few
millimetres from the sunbeam, he smiles and makes that strange deep roaring
sound that lets me know he is fulfilled. His smile is not what most people would
call beautiful as his face is uncommonly big and wide, his eyes badly squinted, his
teeth all at odds with each other leaning this way and that. But I think he's just
lovely and I revel with him in his sunbeam-delight from a distance. Then I take
a soft tissue and walk towards him to wipe drool from his chin before it escapes
and falls onto his clothes.

Rashid is nearly four years old and has one of those rare syndromes that you
need to look up in the medical dictionary, but because I'm trained in education
not medicine, I never quite fully grasp his condition in its entirety. He is partially
sighted, quite deaf, and struggles with his balance and co-ordination. He loves
shiny things and his favourite colour is red, so we've already bought lots of shiny

red things for him to twirl, shake, and flick in the light. He loves his treasure basket and often drags it along the floor of the nursery, dipping in and out to find something shiny, something red. Most of all, he loves chasing sunbeams.

TUESDAY: Absent – bad cough.

WEDNESDAY: Absent

THURSDAY: Office called – he has a chest infection

FRIDAY: Absent

MONDAY: Absent

TUESDAY: Absent. Heard from Gwen in the office, who lives near Rashid's mum, that he's gone into hospital with suspected pneumonia,

WEDNESDAY: 8.30 am. Mike cancels this afternoon's meeting. I ring Rashid's mum to arrange a hospital visit instead to bring in his treasure basket and cards from the children.

On arrival at the ward, I am shown into a waiting room where the nurse explains that Rashid has deteriorated during the morning and they want to move him to another hospital. Our rural hospital just can't cope with his needs and he's on life-support. Rashid's mum, Aisha, comes out to meet me in the waiting room and says I can go in. I hesitate. I hate hospitals: the smell of cleaning agents, the squeaky, shiny floors, the faraway look on people's faces, and the scent of fear.

As I look at Rashid, I feel out of place holding two sparkly red helium-filled Paddington bear balloons, bought on impulse from the shop at the hospital entrance. I look at his corpse-like body lying amidst the whirring of machines, his pale, waxy skin shrouded by his limp black hair on the pillow. There is a cold eeriness around us as the machines pump, whirr, and click.

She opens her eyes one last time and slowly ponders the face of each of her children before giving out her last, long, breath. Then, in response to a deep roar of desolation from the core of my being and the cries of 'No!' emitted from my siblings, the Macmillan nurse[1] comes into the room to check my mother's pulse. She struggles to find anything, then nods to herself. The faintest pulse can still be felt in my mother's neck. The nurse turns to us and says "The last sense to leave us when we die is the sense of hearing, so, if there is anything you want to say to your mum, you still have a few moments. She can hear you."

I step back, tie the balloons to a chair and put down the treasure basket, then walk back to his bedside. I don't really know what to do. This is not what I'd expected. Then, instinctively, I touch his hair and stroke his icy-cold face. [Her hair was fair and her skin was still warm when I last held her in my arms as she let go of all her worldly troubles.] My hand trembles on sensing the coldness.

Hello Rashid, I know you can hear me. I guess you're probably a bit scared in this strange space right now … I'm scared too. But, d'you know what Rashid, this room is full of sunbeams? They're beautiful and they're everywhere. I wonder if you can see them from wherever you are. And the red balloons I brought with me and the cards from the children at nursery are here too. We've all been thinking about you.

Leaning over to stroke his face, I hum one of our nursery songs to him quietly.

A nurse suddenly appears and asks us all to leave to make way for the medical team rushing down the corridor. Rashid is being air-lifted to Cardiff children's hospital as the doctor reckons he won't survive the three-hour ambulance ride it would take to get there.

In the corridor, gentle weeping can be heard as Rashid's mum is consoled by her husband, Malik. Her head is buried, nesting deep in his arms. They are alone. Having fled Lebanon during a time of fighting and conflict some years ago to set up a new life here, they are now far away from their extended family. I hear Aisha's wailing cries from her heart, but I am overwhelmed by my own memories and can't cope. I quietly make my excuse to leave and hug Aisha before I go.

In the carpark, I stand for a few moments with the warmth of the sun on my face as tears well up then quietly disperse down my cheeks onto my clothes. It's early summer and the warmed air has drawn out the scent of the late May blossom on the trees. I pause and then stretch out my hands to touch the sunbeams on the bonnet of my car. I smile, recognising I'm doing what Rashid loves best. I'm touching sunbeams.

Nurseries, brimming with life and activity, also carry the burden of illness and death too; life happens. I've experienced the death of grandparents through illness and old-age, step-brothers killed in motor-cycle accidents, young mothers dying of breast cancer, uncles who committed suicide, dads killed at sea on fishing boats and baby brothers and sisters who touched the earth for only a few moments. But *nothing* prepares you for dealing with this in the raw.

Over the next two months, I receive regular weekly reports from Aisha about Rashid's progress, which I pass on to the nursery team and the children. At the end of every day after everyone has gone home, I sit below Rashid's coat-peg, quietly singing and humming our nursery songs while picturing him. At festival and celebration times, I put whatever we made that day by his place and whenever I catch sight of sunbeams on the wall I place my hand on them as I talk to Rashid in my head, or is it my heart?

Then, after more than two months have passed, the call comes to let me know he's coming back, tomorrow. I dash around the local shops and buy as many red shiny balloons as I can find and, in the morning, I tie them to the fence. As he walks around the corner and comes into view on the path, we all cheer and the children call out his name as they rush to the gate. But I have to step back as tears roll down my face. I turn once more to touch his coat-peg. I can feel my body reverberating, pulsing with so many emotions: anguish, joy, grief, loss, thankfulness. Then I walk towards the nursery kitchen to fetch the flour and eggs: We're making a cake today to celebrate Rashid's return, so there's no time to stand and stare.

At snack-time, sitting between Rashid and Jonathan, I'm startled as Rashid suddenly grabs my hair, crashing his head into mine with a firm grip on my neck and hair. I can't disentangle his fingers and he refuses to let go. Magda, a colleague, quickly intervenes to remove Rashid's fingers one by one from my hair, but is unsuccessful and, despite pleas from me and shrieks of pain, he won't let go. So, eventually, I resolve to sit quietly and accept the fate of my head.

"What do you want Rashid? Do you want to play a game?" I ask.

He holds onto my head tightly, very tightly and then it happens. I hear a quiet, barely audible sound. Rashid is quietly humming some tones and I can hear them *inside* my head. Then he stops. Silence. He starts humming again with random tones and they penetrate my head and spine and I begin to tingle as I '*get*' what he's doing. I gently hum random notes back. He hoots loudly and giggles in response, rocking back and forth taking my head along. Then, gripping my head even more forcefully, he begins humming again. For several minutes, we exchange our tones. Then I hum one of our nursery songs and he gently strokes my face with one hand, holding my head tightly with the other. Then he sits quietly for a moment before letting my head go. I sit still then give him a hug. He knows I understand and I humbly accept this invitation into his world – though not without pain! Then I pause and wonder … did he hear me at the end of every day?

Embodied knots: inclusion, 'listening', loss, wordless storytelling

Watching Rashid was always a delight because he took such pleasure in everything he did. I sorely missed his presence during his illness and it didn't feel right to simply forget about him during his hospital stay. As we practised 'keeping children in mind,' routinely letting them know throughout the day that we were there for them, it felt quite natural to sit down at the end of the day and tell him what we had been doing. I often felt his presence, a delicate sort of warmth, and somehow this quiet time 'with him' helped me to come to terms with the loss of my mother. I had returned to nursery a few days after her funeral but never really felt I'd had time to grieve properly and now Rashid was helping me to do that. In effect, he became my teacher and healer.

The intimate incursion into Rashid's resonating inner world came as a complete surprise. He wasn't a touchy-feely sort of child at all, so his intimacy and physical contact was unexpected. I've often wondered why he chose to do that, for he never did it again, and I wondered if he was telling me he knew what I'd been doing during his illness, but of course I can't be sure. The experience with him brought home to me the richness of every child's inner life and the multiple ways of communicating and storytelling with another human being, as well as the power of simple, loving thoughts. I was deeply moved by the invitation to enter his inner world and humbled by it. It felt as though he was telling me 'I see you. I hear you. I know you. This is my world, your world, our world.'

Note

1 Macmillan nurses work in palliative care in the UK.

6

A TALE OF TWO HALVES AND MORE

Considering difference and listening

Asking, I find You
a far cry from this blinding
light. Lead, I'll follow

(Thewless, 2016)

9.30	Owen is lying on the beach horizontally, digging with his hands like the claws on a digger. He feels the sand with his fingers and now and then pauses to stroke his thumbs over his other sand-covered fingers. Owen is playing alone. He is silent	Marcus lies down beside the play basket and takes out the *Thomas the Tank Engine* wooden toys. He lines them up
9.45	Using a spade, Owen constructs a mound of sand then sprinkles it with dry sand from a height. He pats the sand carefully then rests his face on the mound and closes his eyes. Then using both hands he sculpts an embankment around the mound, carefully moulding it and patting it from one side then the other. It grows to over three metres long	Marcus is lying on the floor making train sounds; his eyes are very close to the trains. He seems to be looking inside the carriages, I think. He is silent
10.00	Owen goes off to see what the big boys are doing.	Marcus is alone and has placed the train track across the floor in a line.

(Continued)

	He crouches down and inspects the huge hole they're digging. He watches in silence then nods before returning to his place where he starts to dig a hole beside the embankment. He quickly returns to see the big boys then heads back to his sand sculpture and gently moves his body slowly over the embankment. He comes to rest and closes his eyes. He is humming quietly	He takes the box and looks carefully at the picture on the cover. Then he takes the track piece by piece and lays it out like the picture. He is silent
10.45	After snack, Owen heads for the little stream. He has a small transparent bucket with him. Crouching by the stream, he puts his right hand in the cold spring water. He doesn't flinch, but holds his hand in the flow dangling his fingers like seaweed in the water	After snack, Marcus continues with the train set, pulling the carriages round and round the track. He makes train sounds
11.00	The sun is sparkling on the water. I wonder if Owen is trying to catch sun-stars as he scoops up water then watches as it trickles down his fingers into the stream. He places his hand in the water and rotates it, extending his fingers. He takes the bucket, fills it with water, then lets the water flow from the bucket back into the stream several times	Marcus is lying on the floor with his eyes up against the carriages. He moves his body with the train around the track, his face touching the carriages. Justine knocks over some wooden bricks nearby. As they clatter down, some fall on Marcus. He shrieks and sticks his fingers in his eyes, pulling his eyelids wide. He goes into the corner of the room
11.30	Owen's body is carefully balanced over the stream as though suspended by a string. I can hear him gently humming a melody. He scoops and splashes water with his hands, trails his fingers across the surface, then plunges his hands deep into the stream with fingers outstretched like stars. He tries to nip the water with a crab-like gesture before rotating his hands through the stream. After twenty minutes, he goes back to his sand sculpture	Marcus is rocking gently back and forth in the corner. His key-worker is talking to him, trying to coax him out. He starts to scream loudly, painfully. The screaming increases, rising to fever pitch. Marcus leaves the room with Alice, his key-worker. She carefully puts on his boots. She takes his arms and places them inside his jacket. He is still shrieking and rocking. Marcus and Alice go outside to the nursery garden
12.00	Owen is lying on his sand sculpture in silence.	Marcus still has his fingers in his eyes, but has stopped shrieking.

He is almost motionless, though occasionally gently creeps his fingers across the sand	He doesn't stop to look at anything in the garden, but when he comes to a halt, he rocks back and forth with eyes closed
12.15 Owen stands up then launches his body into the sand sculpture with a loud hooting sound. He laughs, throws some sand into the air, then runs off to see the big boys again	Marcus stands by the fence. He is motionless and silent

Dream sequence

DREAM: I hear someone calling my name and turn round to see Marcus.

"What are you doing here, Marcus?" I ask, rather stunned.

"I've come to be with you," he replies and smiles. (Marcus is three and a half years old.)

A few moments later. I am standing at the top of a staircase. Looking downstairs. I see a young man, about twenty years old, sitting on a child's plastic ride-on tractor. He is smiling. I begin to descend the stairs and slowly become aware that he looks a bit like Marcus. I stop half-way down the stairs.

EH: Marcus? Marcus is that you?

MARCUS: Yes (*very softly*).

EH: You look amazing! You look so well and … grown up! (*I can't really believe what's happening and am quite perplexed.*)

MARCUS: Thanks. I'm fine, I'm well.

EH: What are you doing here?

MARCUS: I want you to know that I'll be okay. It will be fine. Don't worry.

EH: (*tearful*) But I do worry Marcus. I worry about your pain, suffering … and …

MARCUS: Please don't worry.

[After a tearful pause, I realise that I have an incredible moment of opportunity. I need to ask Marcus some questions.]

EH: Marcus … Marcus, I have a question. Can I ask you a question, please?

MARCUS: Yes, okay. (*He steps off the tractor, walks closer to the bottom of the stairwell then looks up at me.*)

EH: I don't understand Marcus and I'm trying to understand … I don't … I don't understand why you have to be in such pain, struggling to make sense of the world, struggling to communicate, struggling to be with people… I just don't get it. Why does it have to be like this? Why so much pain?

MARCUS: (*steps forward and stands close beside me*) Well… some of us have to mask our gifts at this time because we need people to ask questions and to find us. It's a sacrifice, to help people find their way again. It's how it has to be.

EH: (*I start to cry*) I'm trying so hard to understand… and to help you, but it's not easy …or straightforward and sometimes I just don't know what to do.

MARCUS: You're doing okay, don't worry. I do know how much you care. I know you care.

Marcus fades out of my sight. He's gone and I'm left alone on the stairs.

When I wake up, my face is wet with crying. I go downstairs to sit quietly, to ponder on what's just happened. The picture of Marcus as a young man is simply radiant and I hear his words for several minutes over and over again. I write them down.

Embodied knots: silence, intuition and flow

The observation notes on Marcus (3.5 years) and Owen (3 years) were actually made about ten years apart. It seemed to me on re-reading them that they belonged together.

You could be forgiven for thinking that I've placed these observation notes together to illustrate Marcus' deficits, but that wasn't my intention. I juxtaposed them in the hope that the incredible effort necessary on Marcus' part just to be in the world might be evident, the on-going pain and his attempts to deal with it and the courage needed on a daily basis.

Owen's observation notes exemplify free-flow play on a day-visit to the beach. The duration of his activity and the sensory pleasures of touching and playing with both sand and water are clearly apparent. The deep involvement and engrossment in his play, almost wholly in silence, signals his ability to engage with his imagination and his senses at length, over a sustained period. The absolute joy of his activity was evident from his body language and his facial expressions. He was very peaceful and deeply absorbed throughout and I, in turn, became deeply engrossed in my observations of his activities. I experienced flow.

Likewise, Marcus was deeply absorbed in his play, repetitive like Owen's, but in a different way, and to what extent he enjoyed the sensory experience is difficult to tell. The effect of the sudden and disturbing sound, however, is evident, as is the pain it caused. Being out in the garden was always Marcus' choice whenever he felt anxious.

I tried for many months to gain insight into Marcus' world through my observations. I struggled with the pain I felt he was enduring just to be in the world. It reminded me of an experience I had some years earlier when a roller-towel machine fell off the wall as I was drying my hands in a public toilet. Landing on the bridge of my nose it knocked me out for a few seconds. With stitches on my nose, I went home from the hospital to sleep off a blinding headache but, on waking up, discovered that my olfactory sense, my sense of smell, situated on the bridge of my nose, had become hyper-sensitive. I was unable to cope with the overwhelming smells that invaded my senses: garlic, cooking oils, fabric conditioner, diesel, soap, the dog's breath, perfume, the children's wet jackets, and boots … I hid under the duvet, breathing through my mouth to avoid the smells. I simply couldn't be in the room with anyone else; it was too painful.

After some thirty-six hours or so, my olfactory sense reverted to its normal capacity. I had a bit of insight into Marcus' pain through his hyper-sensitivity to light and sound.

When I had the dream, I was taken aback, especially with his words. I felt perplexed by them but chose to carry these words with me, like a touchstone, in my attempts to find and get to know children and their worlds. Working with Marcus, in short, changed my life. He challenged me to reconfigure what I thought I knew about being in the world, how to be with young children, and how to connect.

7

DOG-EYED

How do children see their world? How do we see them?

> before it recedes
> a tide brings you the present
> of a star-shaped fish
>
> (Thewless, 2009)

The children wanted to investigate dogs after Rachel got one for her seventh birthday, so we invited several unusual dogs and their owners into school: a local farmer brought in Chippy, the sheepdog, who worked on his farm; Mrs. Alexander, a local guide-dog trainer, brought in Oscar; and Ellie's uncle, who volunteered in the local mountain rescue team, brought in Max, who had recently been part of the rescue team that responded to the Lockerbie plane crash disaster. On the last week of our exploration of 'dogs that help us,' Rachel asked if she could bring in Lily, her pup. I agreed. She was very excited and with her mum's help, she brought Lily to school. Just before Rachel's mum came to take the pup home, Rachel asked me if I'd like to pat Lily one last time. Then she said:

RACHEL: You know that a dog has two eyes ...

EH: Usually ... um ...yes... dogs have two eyes, unless they've had an accident or a serious eye illness.

RACHEL: Well, I do *know* that a dog has two eyes because I can see them when the dog's over there (*she points to a distance of about one metre*), but when the dog is close by, like now, (*she strokes Lily's head*) I can only see one side of her head at a time so it looks like she's only got one eye ... but I know that's not true. Funny, isn't it? Don't you think?

EH: Em ... is it always like that? I mean, do you only see one side of Lily close up?

RACHEL: Yes. And when I'm horse riding I have a blind spot, just like the horses. Did you know they have a blind spot?

EH: No, I didn't… tell me about it.

RACHEL: Well, when they get close to a jump, they don't see the poles but jump anyway because the rider guides them. When I get close to the jumps, everything disappears for me too, just as I'm taking off to make the jump, then it all reappears a second later. I don't mind though because I know the poles won't disappear, I know where they are. Me and the horse, we trust each other. We just fly through the air!

EH: So … um…when you're reading, Rachel and the book is close up, can you see everything on the page? Or … is that why you hold the book at a funny angle?

RACHEL: Probably, yeah … sometimes I can only see the beginning and the end of a big word so I have to keep moving the page about. Oh look, here comes mum to take Lily home.

(*Rachel shakes Lily's paw at me, then the class*)

RACHEL: Say 'Bye' to Ms. Henderson, Lily, and my class.

Embodied knots: attachment, challenge, insight

Rachel was a very affectionate and bubbly girl in my primary school class. She had struggled for some time with her reading, writing, and spelling and I had wondered why, as she seemed so bright. It appeared not to bother her that she was behind the others with her literacy skills. She had a busy outdoor life on the farm with her horse and I tried not to make an issue of it. Chatting with me, however, when I had Lily on my lap, changed everything. I suddenly had an insight into her world and the tremendous effort she had to make to 'see' things and still, further, to make sense of it all. I was touched by her conversation and consequently decided to study sensory integration to help me better understand Rachel's world.

Unravelling the knots: difference, listening, inclusion

The section that now follows relates to the knots of the wayfaring line in Chapters 5, 6, and 7.

Difference

To be different, or to make a difference, requires a benchmark against which to be measured, such as a model or norm. Perhaps this is fine when discussing the merits of compost in a garden and its impact on the size of the carrots, or when comparing winter tyres on the car to non-winter tyres and whether they actually help or not in the snow. But when considering human beings, is it right to measure in this way? Disability, as the word suggests, is a deficit. The prefix 'dis' expresses "negation" or denotes "reversal or absence of an action or state" (Soanes and Stevenson, 2008, p. 407). Disability is generally understood to mean "a physical or mental condition that limits a person's movements, senses, or activity … a disadvantage or handicap" (ibid). Difference is a key feature of the last three stories, and I now want to explore ways of going beyond "outlived habits and attitudes" (Semetsky, 2012, p. 50) and "outlived model(s)" (p. 47) in our understanding of difference. In order to gain a more critical understanding of what disability means, I will also turn to the work of Goodley (2014).

On average

The question of whether disability is an individual issue or a social problem is part of a current and fluid debate impacting on the lives of those labelled 'disabled.' Current UK Government criteria for disability benefits and services in the UK are hierarchically rated: "moderate, substantial or critical" (Oliver, 2013, p. 1,026) inherent within which is the assumption that some disabilities are more worthy and deserving than others.

Just over thirty years ago, Oliver (2013) created a social model that turned the understanding of disability, as an individual plight, on its head. Suggesting that disability was not an individual issue but that there were "disabling barriers" (p. 1,025) faced by some people that needed to be addressed and eradicated initially drew criticism to Oliver's radical concept. Eventually these criticisms were largely dispelled by the actions of collective groups as they campaigned together on their rights. This culminated in legislation that required changes to public transport and buildings, to create easier access for disabled people, and legislation to protect them from discrimination. Current austerity measures, however, have seen the present Conservative Government in the UK fall quiet on the issue of eradicating barriers and a growing return to individualising the issue of disability. But, as Oliver also pointed out, little actually changed within education in response to the 'social model' and disabled children continued to be treated as individuals with issues and challenges.

Riddell (2009) recognises the place of disability within the inclusion discourse that has been part of "policy orthodoxy" (p. 289) since 2000. In 2004, the *Education (Additional Support for Learning) (Scotland) Act* (2004), commonly referred to as the ASL Act, gave responsibility to local authorities to both identify and address the learning needs of children who needed extra support (Scottish Executive, 2004a). The ASL Act introduced new terminology, moving away from the more common understanding of disability or special needs to encompass a wider range of needs, both short and long term, such as bullying, bereavement or illness; additional support needs (ASN).

Implementation of the Act would seem to signal that children with ASN should be treated equally to other children. However, Riddell (2009) indicates that parents have struggled on behalf of their children to achieve their rights, often being met with hostility. Compounding the challenges faced, she notes that resources have gone disproportionately to boys with dyslexia from backgrounds that are more financially favourable than their peers from disadvantaged homes, leading Riddell to state that "sharp-elbowed middle class" parents (p. 292) employed more successful strategies. Riddell contests that the Government's strategy to apply "weak forms of redistribution and recognition" (p. 294), which ultimately do little to challenge education, continues to "reproduce, rather than undermine, existing inequalities" (ibid). It points to a perception that children's needs should be addressed individually and the education system need not change as children will be supported to manage within it. In other words, they will be assisted to be as 'normal' as possible within a system underpinned by assumptions and values around normality.

Beyond average

As Goodley (2014, p. 7) reflects, the social model was and is "inspirational" and benefited the lives of many people with disabilities. It changed the view of "disability-as-impairment" (a classic medicalising strategy) to "disability-as-oppression," a socio-political view (ibid). The social model challenged and continues to challenge the "processes of *disablement*: social, economic and cultural barriers that prevent people with impairments from living a life like their non-impaired brothers and sisters" (ibid). ASN comes in many forms, for example, impairments to eyesight, dyslexia, mobility difficulties, and mental health issues such as depression.

More recently, the debate has moved on to interrogating political discourses, using a critical lens, to elicit the assumptions and concepts that still need to be expunged if those with disabilities are to be seen as whole human beings and not deficits. At the root of some of the issues lies the notion that there is an ideal body, a normal body, a socially acceptable body, building the notion of "ableism", which Goodley considers affords the possibility to then identify "disablism" (p. xii).

Within the current climate of neoliberal politics, which expounds the value of each individual to the nation as an economic unit, being dis/abled may lead to being seen as a threat to global capitalism through need and deficit. As Goodley states, "The neoliberal-able education system excludes those who are unable to step up to ableist demands" (p. 54) at variance with the notion that education should be freeing and liberating. What follows now is a consideration of the role of education in the lives of those considered disabled (or disadvantaged) and possible ways of going beyond the current rhetoric.

Cry freedom

A discourse on the vital role of education in helping liberate those bound by poverty or disadvantage is attributed to Freire (1972), who contests the right of governments to control and suppress their people through an education system that nurtures dependency and compliance. Freire's thesis is predicated on the concept that most education systems are based on the notion of accumulation, or banking, in which students are discouraged from being active agents in their learning, instead accumulating knowledge uncritically. Failure to provide the opportunity to explore and be active in learning denies the student the possibility of learning how to learn, how to problem-solve, and ultimately the capacity to develop their own opinions and speak for themselves with their own voice. Learning that recognises the importance of problem-solving is, according to Freire, one that recognises the fluidity and on-going process of learning and becoming. "Education is thus constantly remade in the praxis" (p. 57), which Freire defines as "humanist and liberating" (p. 58). The "banking method" (p. 57) of education, on the other hand, is deterministic and denies transformation of the individual through oppression, subsequently negating the "ontological vocation to be more fully human" (p. 48). Freire asserts that love is "commitment to other men" (p. 62) and that both love and courage are needed to create the "foundation of dialogue" (p. 62), a necessary attribute to transformation.

Education, as a liberatory project, is acclaimed by other writers, including bell hooks (1994, p. 53), who asserts that Freire recognised the needs of those most "disenfranchised" in society and subject to oppression. Similarly, Giroux (2002) asserts that discourses in "democracy, political agency, and pedagogy" (p. 103) must be viewed collectively if we are to engender an education underpinned by hope.

As Goodley (2014) asserts, "disablism" is a form of oppression exerted by a society that moves to "exclude, eradicate and neutralize those individuals, bodies, minds and community practices that fail to fit the capitalist imperative" (p. xi). *Disablism* exists because the concept or view of *ableism* is the breeding ground for "paranoia, confusion, fear and inadequacy" (p. xi) as the ideal body or mind is actually something unachievable. What may seem to have been a "benign" concept of ability initially has also spawned a shadow that, in turn, has marginalised those that do not fit the ideals of ableism (p. xii).

Moving from a political to an ethical and social stance, leading the discourse in a new direction, is discussed in the following section.

A change in perspective

In order to create a form of education that has the potential to fully respect the individuality of children with ASN or disabilities, and therefore enable transformation, needs a radical approach. We need to break out of "old outlived habits and attitudes" (Semetsky, 2012, p. 50) if we are to reach new perceptions.

Several scholars attest to the importance of liminal and relational spaces in helping children/students to be who they want/need to be, situated within transformative practices (Adami, 2015; Hoveid and Finne, 2015; Todd, 2015; Batchelor, 2012). Transformation as a concept is not new in education. It dates back to ancient Greek times and is firmly located within the relational space between teacher and pupil, expanding the "borders of our self-understanding" (Todd, 2015, p. 57). As Todd puts it, transformation is the "pedagogical act of living *par excellence*" (ibid) and it resides at the core of educational intent. With the premise that human beings are "unfinished, uncompleted beings in and with a likewise unfinished reality" in the process of "becoming," Freire (1972, p. 57) considers an awareness of this "incompleteness" (ibid) to be at the heart of the foundation stone of education.

Adopting a transformational stance, through the affordances within liminal spaces (see discursive space after 'A silence louder than words' in Chapter 2), consequently frees practitioners to re-view their practices through a new lens, to include the more "subtle, unnameable dimensions" (Todd, 2015, p. 69) of life within practice. This does not necessitate abandoning current practices by retracting from "academic judgements" (p. 69), or the role played by practitioners in the socialisation of children, but enables engagement with something beyond the standard practices in which we engage, if we consider that education can be transformational.

Respect for children and 'listening' to them within a relational space, helps to reimagine relationships and a new "possibility for interpretation of pedagogical practices" (Hoveid and Finne, 2015, p. 77). However, it is important to recognise that both children and practitioners are unique and that children are dependent on practitioners who are located within historical, cultural, and social spaces. Freedom, therefore, is relational, both within micro and macro contexts, and is "under constant re-negotiation" (Adami, 2015, p. 139).

Revisiting an ethic of care

Noddings' ethic of care (see discursive space after 'Listening to Lola' in Chapter 4) provides Semetsky (2012) with the springboard for a consideration of a new ethic for modern times. Utilising the lens of philosophers Deleuze and Guattari (1987), Semetsky extends the concept of an ethic of care, indicating that Noddings' concept is situated within a relational space, predicated on our awareness of "moral interdependence, that is, self-becoming-other by means of entering into another person's frame of reference and taking upon oneself the other perspective" (p. 54). Semetsky considers a theory of care enables us to view the world "via *relations* and *caring* because in the framework of care theory it is a relation (and not an individual agent) that is ontologically and ethically basic" (ibid). Consequently, Semetsky's proposal for an "ethics of integration" (p. 57) foregrounds the importance of relationships and interdependence at many levels, but essentially the notion that integrating "the other" through our life experiences, is a way of creating the building blocks for an "inclusive education" (p. 56).

Perhaps this is more easily understood as a form of deep empathy that can be subsumed into the working practices of a practitioner after first developing the potential of viewing the experience of the other 'from the inside?' Early years practitioners are more than halfway there, I would suggest, as good working practice is built on observations. Semetsky encourages us to go one step further, to view what we observe as if deep within ourselves and not as a practice simply for external consideration. As a contribution to inclusion, Goodley (2014, p. 113) suggests Semetsky's proposal encourages practitioners to "become-Other," which enriches the development of a caring pedagogy that recognises "caring becomings" (p. 114).

Rashid, Marcus, and Rachel, *my teachers*, took me inside their world and helped me begin to develop a "caring becoming(s)" (p. 114) relationship with each of them, introducing me to an "ethics of integration" (p. 57).

Guerillas on the margin

The inclusion of children with ASN into schools has, as Riddell noted, at times been met with hostility, their parents often being treated as "unwelcome customers" (2009, p. 294). Perhaps the perceived threat of change is too much for some teachers and practitioners? Likewise, the parents of some children resisted the change, fearing their children's needs would not be met.

Building on a metaphor that he introduced elsewhere, Goodley (2014, p. 104) draws the location of guerrillas into the debate as those on the margin who "enter the landscape, plant some ideas and watch what happens. Disabled kids are guerrillas encroaching upon education." As a provocative thought, this suggests something of a sacrifice on the part of those children who have been and to some degree remain marginalised, as well as attesting to the power of their agency and resonates with my dream sequence, outlined in Chapter 6: 'A tale of two halves,' with Marcus. It also raises the possibility that working with disabled children in education challenges the very project that is education as:

> Pedagogies are found lacking and educational settings are revealed to be horribly instrumental. Disability exposes the failings of educational in-stitutions that still, after years of disability advocacy and activism, fail to anticipate their responsibilities to a wide body of students and to the varied bodies of individual learners. Being surrounded by such failings-and our candid appreciation of their failings-provokes action.
>
> *(Goodley, 2014, p. 104)*

Goodley, resonating with a conference participant's question asks: "How can we be humbled by disability?" (ibid) to which I respond next.

A quiet, revolutionary revelation

My encounters with Marcus, Rachel, and Rashid stripped back my humanity to its core, making me challenge my assumptions and my "un/conscious ideals around normality" (Goodley, 2014, p. 85). Often I felt uncertain about what to do, how to help them and how to understand them, while experiencing my own frailties and anxieties about my in/competence and professionalism. So, I did what I do best and I watched, attuning myself to their world and listened, daily. On a continuous basis, they humbled me as I witnessed them trying to make sense of their world, my world, our world. Consequently, their gift was to make me a far better human being for, as I journeyed with them, I watched in awe of their courage and tenacity to simply *be* in an ever hardening, excluding world. Slowly, they revolutionised my world, from the margins, inside; they *were* my teachers.

PART III
Autoethnography at work

8

WORKING WITH AUTOETHNOGRAPHY

Finding my voice — considerations of methodology

Living, telling, retelling, and reliving mark the qualities of a life.
(Clandinin and Connelly, 2000, p. 187)

When writing this chapter, I experienced discomfort. I wasn't sure where to begin and felt restless. How could I share this experience of actually finding a way to share my stories, my voice, and why was it so vital for me to write these stories at all? Perhaps my personal situation as a latecomer to the world of academia was the problem. I simply didn't fit in and could not find a connection to most paradigms and methodologies. I felt they would rob me of the immediacy of what I wanted to convey and so, ultimately, I had to search to find my fit; to find a way that would not dilute my voice, my stories, my need to make sense of my world. Pondering the mess on my desk, something began to happen...

Bubbling up

I look at the papers scattered all over my desk and scan several fragments in desperation trying to locate what it is that I need for this chapter. Where to begin? I find a note to myself, scribbled with a fragment from Palmer's (2007) book: "The work required to 'know thyself' is neither selfish nor narcissistic ... Good teaching requires self-knowledge: it is a secret hidden in plain sight" (Palmer, 2007, p. 3). Something bubbles up inside. Right, maybe this is what I need to attend to. I pick up my notes and read Palmer again: "good teaching cannot be reduced to technique; good teaching comes from the identity and integrity of the teacher" (p. 10). Okay, identity. Didn't Osgood (2012) say something about that? Ah... here it is on her last page... we need to "make space to 'hear the stories' of those that make up the nursery workforce and to act upon constructions of '*professionalism from within*'" (p. 154, my italics). Yes... identity again and the importance of storying. I continue to scrabble through layers of documents and fragments of paper littering my table then find another note referring to Nutbrown's (2011) work. My scribbled note states: *CN considers the autoethnographic process has "identity" at its core* (Nutbrown, 2011, p. 235). So ... I guess I need to say something more about identity? I ponder for a while on this and reflect on my stories then – for some unknown reason – I start to move towards the bookshelf ...

Conversations with books from within

I pull five books with browning pages down from my bookshelf, two of which are well worn with creased covers and dog-eared pages. While pondering their significance, and their smell, the voice of my undergraduate self begins to speak from the books. We begin to chat. I have called her '75,' not an attractive name, I know, but it helps me to locate her in 1975 because that's where she resides.

EH: So, what's the significance of these books then? Why on earth did I just leap up and fetch them?

75: Well, do you remember the incredibly tight budget I was living on in 1975?

EH: Yes, I do indeed.

75: Well, I splashed out a bit on books that inspired me and you're holding them now. I got a bit carried away by them. I think this is the order I bought them in: Freire, 1972, *Pedagogy of the oppressed,* which cost 60p; Kellmer Pringle, 1975, *The needs of children,* £1.95. Blimey, that almost broke the bank as I was living on a weekly budget of £5. Piaget, 1973, *The child's conception of the world,* £1.50; Hudson, 1967, *Contrary Imaginations,* cheap at 40p; Wedge and Prosser, 1973, *Born to fail?* 65p. None of them were on the course reading list, but they all spoke to me and somehow gave my life a sense of meaning and coherence ...

Pause – silence...

EH: Blimey, they've travelled with me through numerous 'flittings'[1] and a lifetime of challenge. But what's that got to do with this book?

75: Can't you see it? (Long pause) They pre-scribed your professional journey?

EH: What? Hmm, did they? Okay, let me think about this for a moment. Freire spoke to me of the fight against oppression and the need for freedom. Kellmer Pringle contextualised my experience of growing up in a working-class family and its situated challenges. Piaget's book on how children conceive of the world was insightful and drew me ever inwards to imagining how to make children's experiences even greater, wider, full of mystery, and awe. Hudson helped me to understand myself a bit better through my left-handedness and my somewhat different way of seeing things. I had a tendency to think 'outside the box' and so never felt like I fitted in academically. But Wedge and Prosser's book blew me away because it gave me my first insight into the bigger picture around poverty. My first experience of a grand narrative! It was a bit depressing reading their book, though, because it told me that poverty was a killer. It affected everything: health, educational outcomes, and behaviour. I remember understanding their book as an insider, yet somehow I also felt guilty too, like I'd suddenly become an outsider. I see that I underlined a whole paragraph on page 55:

> Only one in 25 of the disadvantaged was middle-class; the overwhelming majority was working-class. Hence part of their failure to 'succeed' arises from the differences between their own language, values, and experiences of life and these implicitly or explicitly put forward by the school.

(I flick through to the end of the book and read their concluding words aloud.)

EH: Listen! Page 61, this is how they end the book:

> If children are indeed our country's investment in the future, then everyone has a stake in their welfare. Reducing the material inequalities that help to cripple the life chances of disadvantaged children should have an urgent priority. *Do we mind if children grow up in bad housing when we could do something about it? Do we mind the stress caused by low incomes when we could afford to change it?*
> *As a society do we really care sufficiently about our children to reduce drastically the hardships of their families? Do we care that so many are born to fail?*

75: Hmmm. (Pause).

EH: These words could have been written yesterday. It seems that not much has changed. Power still dictates. Wealth divides. So, what's the point? (My head sinks into my hands.)

75: Well … you're still struggling with the vestiges of modernity, aren't you, so you just have to keep going.

EH: Yes, you're right. (Pause) Oh, wait a minute… you're going … I can feel you're going… wait, please! I want to say thanks for hanging around all this time. You've saved me so many times from packing in my job and giving up. Honestly. I couldn't have got through this without you and these books!

75: I'm always here, in between heartbeats. But would you please stop calling me 75? I don't like it and I already have a name. My name is Hope.

★★★

Was this the inner driver of my stories? Was it hope? Was I struggling with these life events because I had almost lost hope and needed to find a paradigm and a methodology that would help me express this frustration and despair?

Pondering the children and their stories drew them closer to me. I could hear their voices: Ruby's whispers, Darren's lisping and shouting, Marcus' wailing. My skin began to tingle. I could smell the children too. Does that sound odd, to smell children? Darren always smelled of a well-known brand of laundry liquid, but Ruby, well, Ruby didn't smell of that so much as the smell of fear and death. Perhaps that's why she had haunted me because I just couldn't accept that a child so young could, somehow, emit that scent. It shouldn't be possible. It's not acceptable, is it? But how could I express this to others, knowing that practitioners keep their silence, often to protect themselves?

Searching for a research paradigm and methodology to embrace my children and my stories

Research paradigms are predicated on belief systems about truth and to what extent the world can be known. I needed a paradigm that would allow me to speak my inner voice while affording the chance to maintain my need for coherence, but it seemed that some paradigms precluded that.

The adoption of constructivism, postmodern and post-structural paradigms, complexity and quantum theories in research go beyond the bounds and strictures of more traditional research paradigms, challenging accepted knowledge and beliefs about how life is structured and whether there is an objective truth to be found and told. Such a departure from long-held ontological and epistemological beliefs, through the adoption of newer, creative methodologies such as autoethnography, has created a "hairline fracture in the academic foundation" (Pelias, 2005, p. 417), causing tremors within the research community. Perhaps this in itself is an attraction for researchers and writers, like me, seeking to speak differently and about difference, feeling the exclusion of our voices from conventional research? Feeling like we belong in the crack?

However, poststructuralism's emphasis on promoting fragmentation in writing (Crotty, 1998) seems to me to preclude any sense of coherence. Instead, it emphasises a series of possible becomings. While this may avert tendencies towards reductionism in narrative writing, it also fails to develop unity and therefore any sense of intentionality and is a matter contested by some writers, particularly those who emphasise that intention is underpinned by an emotion and emotion lies at the core of our being human. Adding to this, Galligan (2000) emphasises the need for human beings to integrate their inner and outer worlds to create a sense of well-being, while Gill (2014, p. 22), stressing "that this postmodern 'playfulness' can risk making existence meaningless," questions whether a postmodern self can be responsible for actions.

Coherence

The concept of coherence is central to the work of Antonovsky (1993), who posits that human beings function within a world that is increasingly complex. As complexity increases, so does the possibility for tensions within an individual as well as between people and between individuals and "suprasystems" (p. 970). Consequently, "noise" (ibid) may supersede information, making it difficult for individuals to process information and therefore impede their ability to make sense of life. In turn, this affects their sense of well-being for at our core is the need for meaning-making and coherence.

Perhaps the visceral reaction we experience when our identity and sense of coherence is challenged is indication of our need to engage in creating a new picture of ourselves before we dissolve the other, in order to maintain coherence? It may be an indication that we are, albeit at times subconsciously, in touch with the very pulse of our being-ness or ipseity. When we forget ourselves, like children at play, we embrace a "condition of complete simplicity," which for Elliot (1989) is one way to describe love. But change and challenge disturbs this deep flow of being, creating tension and awareness, possibly leading to embodied pain. A challenge to our notion of 'self' wakes us up, painfully, and demands renegotiation.

My adoption of Ingold's (2007) wayfaring line and knots is indication of how I have constructed my own "picture to live by" (Chopra and Tanzi, 2012), my stories illustrating times when I had to let go of one picture and embrace another; my attempt to maintain a sense of coherence. With the knowledge that we are ever in a process of becoming, "knotting is the fundamental principle of coherence" (Ingold, 2007, p. 14) that averts formlessness. Our narratives give us a sense of "who we are, how we have become and where we are heading" (Gill, 2014, p. 37). The embodied knots in this book reveal moments of challenge, pain and confusion – a call for change, and a need to rebuild my picture, assess who and what I am. But these knots are also there to remind me that this is who I was, reflected through who I am (now), providing insight and sustenance to inform what I might dare to be in the future.

Learning, as Claxton (1999) tells us, takes place "close to the emotional point where challenge may tip into threat" (p. 56), indicating that a degree of resilience is necessary in order to "tolerate strangeness" (p. 331). However, what Antonovsky (1993) highlights is the high degree of complexity currently faced by many people that may feel overwhelming. Consequently, the challenge of maintaining coherence, necessary for learning to take place, may go beyond an individual's resilience as the "noise" (p. 970) may become increasingly disturbing.

Such dissonance in the life of a practitioner may then become an internalised, embodied struggle between "care of the self against duty to others" (Ball, 2003, p. 216), a balancing act which some simply cannot manage or sustain. Autoethnographic narratives play an important role here by inviting the reader inside the inner landscape of a practitioner to experience it for themselves.

Threads of meaning and the wayfaring line

Witkin (2014b), writing in social work, aptly states:

> It is hard to live in a random universe. We need to make sense of our lives, to discover (or generate) a thread that seems to hold together the variegated

tapestry of our experiences. When we have such a thread, we protect it. When it is frayed or cut, we attempt to repair it or find a new one. Social workers and other helping professions often work with people whose life tapestries are barely holding together. By understanding the complexities of change, I believe we might better assist them in repairing or, if necessary, creating a new tapestry of their lives.

(p. 312)

Early years practitioners, engaging with young children, are responsible for up-building a sense of identity with the children in their care, helping them to make sense of life. Some children, like those in my stories, are vulnerable and in need of a thread to hold on to, a sense of attachment and belonging. I felt that need too.

The crafting of our many selves, however, is not a simple linear process and Kondo (1990) has suggested that "western cultural baggage" (1990, p. 24), predicated on a division between the interior self and the outside world, is at the root of our struggle to understand 'self.' Autoethnographic narratives, however, speak "into the *mind/body split*" (Pelias, 2011, p. 663) from an embodied presence, enabling writers to speak about such issues as violence, trauma, and illness from an affective stance. Positioning the researcher's body at the heart of the research affords engagement with a broader and more holistic picture – potent and vibrant – filled with immediacy, researcher agency, and the power to effect change.

Performative autoethnography

Finding a way to illustrate becoming, or "self-making" (Ingold, 2015, p. 156), led me to performative autoethnography, one of several autoethnographies, that advocated (amongst other things) juxtaposing relevant texts within the writing, such as diary entries, government documents, extracts from research articles or cultural texts, to create a multi-dimensional textual space, filled with a "chorus of discordant voices" (Denzin, 2006, p. 433). The concomitant relational space between individuals and others, elicited by the texts, creates something akin to a three-dimensional vibrant space, illustrating and honouring what Jackson and Mazzei call the "becoming 'I'" (2008, p. 305); a vibrant 'self' in the making that extends beyond the limitations and illusion of a "unidimensional" self (Clandinin and Connelly, 2000, p. 147). Such a methodology upholds both the assertions of post-structuralism and the becoming 'self' of a practitioner on their professional journey, as well as avoiding linear narratives that tend to reify the lives of practitioners. It also averts creating a "Hollywood plot" (p. 181), which, like a good fairy tale, ends well, as the multi-dimensional text enables the reader to come to their own view of the events in the narratives.

With no attempt to share a 'truth' in autoethnographic narratives, there is a chance instead to interrogate fragmented narratives, choosing "failed practices" or "uncertain, ungrounded and thus fragile tellings" (Jackson and Mazzei, 2008,

p. 314) to illustrate the becoming 'I.' Through troubling the authority of the writer, decentring the narrative 'I', and using fragmented texts, the biographical illusion of a stable 'self' can be averted and a platform for multiple voices is created (Denzin, 2014a). This was my way forward and my thread, for now I had a methodology that enabled me to work with fragmented becoming 'selves' while simultaneously adhering to my own need to speak of coherence and meaning-making. I concur with writers such as Goodson (2014), who stated that "discontinuities of self" (p. 132), such as those elicited through poststructural and critical writing, can be situated alongside continuity in the research context, while continuing to question the notion that we are "just a shifting set of multiple selves reproduced differently" (ibid). Performative autoethnography, as summed up by Spry (2001), afforded me the chance to do this, providing:

> a space for the emancipation of the voice and body from homogenizing knowledge production and academic discourse structures, thereby articulating the intersections of peoples and culture through the inner sanctions of the always migratory identity.
>
> *(p. 727)*

Drawing out the body "from the shadows of academe (to) consciously interrogate it into the process and production of knowledge" (p. 725), as Spry asserts, renders the body as a research site, an "enfleshed methodology" (p. 726). The body, long absent from research, in turn becomes "the 'breath' of the performative autoethnographer" (Spry, 2011a, p. 502). Emotions, 'felt' moments, intuitions, dreams, sensory experiences, "visceral prompt(s)" (Hickey-Moody, 2013, p. 79), can all be related through the body and the researcher's experiences into the research context, creating deep insight into the lived experiences of a practitioner. Of course, this may be deemed a threat by anyone wishing to maintain the status quo, but to stifle research itself leads to what Sparkes and Smith (2009) have termed an "ontological stagnation" (p. 496) and is it not imperative that we seek to "make space to 'hear the stories' of those that make up the nursery workforce, to act upon constructions of '*professionalism from within*'" (Osgood, 2012, p. 154, italics added) – to hear practitioners' inner stories and their inner journeying?

Deep listening

Within some cultures, there is an acknowledgement of the deep inter-relational aspect of all things and of our interdependence. Ingold (2015) cites the Tlingit people of the northwest Pacific Coast and their relationship with glaciers, which they perceive as the living embodiment of "sound, light and feeling" (p. 82). In turn, it is these qualities that define what a glacier is – its "sonority, luminosity and palpability" (ibid); a glacier is not simply an object, it is alive. This deep, living relationship between the glacier and the Tlingit involves a "coiling over"

(p. 86) of observer and observed in which they are one and interrelated, making it difficult to see where the Tlingit ends and the glacier begins. If we apply this to the autoethnographic narratives in this book, we might ask, where does the practitioner end and the child begin? Do they breathe with another? Do they resonate together? What might that look like?

Catching dreams

In this book, I have drawn on a variety of embodied experiences to illustrate the holistic engagement of my 'self' within each of my stories, acknowledging the value of what Hydén (2013) terms the "heated" body's engagement in the stories rather than the "'cool' cognitive process" (p. 127). The inclusion of a dream, which affected me deeply (see 'A tale of two halves and more' in Chapter 6), signals how embodiment, even at an unconscious level, can further enrich our understanding of the human condition (Poulos, 2006). "Unbeknown" knowledge (Uotinen, 2011, p. 1,307), including ways of knowing that are not predicated on being conscious, such as through anaesthesia or coma, is "unfiltered, raw knowledge that is produced by our body and our senses" (p. 1312). Because of its "hidden nature" (p. 1,308), such knowledge has been viewed with suspicion in research, illustrating how culture affects what we consider to be relevant knowledge.

Within the Aboriginal culture, for example, dreams, another form of unconscious knowledge, are "integrated into everyday life with immediacy of meaning" (Balogh, 2010), something not generally understood in the western world. Yet dreams are "another instance of the creative self" (Kirtsoglou, 2010, p. 332) and should be seen as part of the continuity of understanding the social, emotional, cognitive embodied 'self.' Furthermore, as Miškolci (2015) asserts, dreams like any other form of data can be viewed through a "theoretical interpretive framework" (p. 80) and, I argue, add to the multiple layers of 'self' within autoethnographic texts, thereby augmenting Denzin's "chorus of discordant voices" (2006, p. 433). Through incorporating both our wakeful day consciousness and our unconscious life, we can augment the breadth of multiple interpretations possible, in a given text, incorporating what St. Pierre (2011) calls "transgressive data" and "emotional data" (p. 621).

It is the exclusion in general, I believe, of embodied research that has ultimately marginalised early years work in research. The current trend in research to include emotion, affect, dreamwork, and sensory experience will hopefully create pathways to enabling greater discussion of embodied work in early years settings. As my stories illustrate, there is a pressing need to understand the complexity of caring work more than ever before and practitioners, engaging in autoethnography that demands cognitive and affective awareness (Pelias, 2015), can both reclaim and illuminate the tacit knowledge and practical wisdom embedded in our praxis.

Writing and re:membering

Qualitative researchers generally use a variety of empirical sources in their research such as journals, artefacts, observations, letters, personal experiences, memory boxes, and autobiographical writing. Similarly autoethnographic narratives can be drawn from such materials but, in the main, they are memoried events or experiences.

My stories were crafted from experiences and events throughout my career, prompted by asking myself three key questions:

- What does it feel like to engage in the complexities of early childhood education and care from the inside?
- What dilemmas were faced when working in an early years setting?
- What helped maintain a connection to my own values in the face of professional challenge?

I sat down to ponder which events, and therefore which stories, I should tell.

In a quiet room, I began by "re:member(*ing*)" (Brogden, 2008, p. 855, my italics) some of the events that had troubled me, bringing them back to mind, feeling and re-imagining the contexts: the weather, the season, the people, what they wore, what they smelled like. One of my first and clearest memories was tactile and involved walking back to nursery holding Lola's hand after watching the two white rabbits (see Chapter 1). The air was cold and the wind whipped through my hair several times. Lola's hand was small and I could sense her strength, yet although her grip was strong, it seemed to lack flexibility; the bones of her hand felt welded together and hard. In my heart, I could still feel the intensity of the moment and the 'we-ness' of our journey.

Once the process of 're:member(ing)' began, the stories took on their own life, becoming alive in my imagination, my memory and in my body, with consequent aches, tears, and laughter.

Brogden (2008, p. 855) highlights the importance of artefacts in "re:member(ing)" events from the past, but also their value as a tool to further questioning, asking "How does this artefact reflect ways in which you, as autoethnographer, are produced?" (Brogden, 2010, p. 375). Within this book, several artefacts were used in "re:member(ing)," including a photo, notebooks and a poem. What does the poem of Darren say about me as a practitioner? Why did I keep the photo Ruby gave me as a present?[2] However, most stories were triggered by memories, embodied memories, raising the question to what extent memory can be trusted when researching. All stories, according to Riessman (2008), reflect memory's power to "remember, forget, neglect, and amplify moments in the stream of experience" (p. 29). As O'Donohue (2010, p. 155) writes:

> Memoria is the harvester and harvest of transfigured experience. Deep in the silent layers of selfhood, the coagulation of memoria are at work. It is

because of this subtle integration of self and life that there is the possibility of any continuity in experience.

When Clough (2004b) stated, "… we do not come innocent to a task or situation of events" (p. 374), he referred to the fact that we each come with our intentions and values to our task of writing. Autoethnographic writers, like other writers and researchers, may seek to capitalise on their research and therefore the choice of stories and portrayal of the writer should be interrogated. Subsequently, as Pelias has suggested, we should be "suspicious of the tales we tell" (2015, p. 609) and consider our ethical and moral obligations to others.

Notes

1 Scots term for 'house move'
2 NB. Legislation and regulations on the keeping of personal data are now very different and preclude keeping such objects at home.

9

BEYOND NARRATIVES AND SOLIPSISM TO ETHICAL KNOWING

Ethics and self-care

While the instability of 'self' and identity could be regarded, by some, as impinging detrimentally on research, making it unreliable, insecure, and questionable, it is to this juncture of 'selves' that Davies (1999) and Reed-Danahay (1997) draw our attention. They argue that it is through the "multiple nature of selfhood" (p. 3) that innovative writing can inform readers about social life in greater depth, identifying both a platform for the autoethnographic scholar and an incentive.

A key strength of autoethnographic research is generally viewed as the possibility it affords researchers to critique the positioning of 'self' and others in society (Spry, 2001), by generating multiple voices within an event. Narratives, starting from experience as opposed to theory, in essence explore the space in which individual lives intersect with others. However, if they are overly self-indulgent, lacking any degree of context within which the reader can situate them, they won't change anything and instead run the risk of being deemed solipsistic. The counterpoint to this argument, however, is that autoethnographic narratives deepen our self-understanding while making a valid contribution to our understanding of social life itself (Sparkes, 2013). Context, however, is both vital and complex. It impacts on how and what writers might speak, as Sermijn et al. (2008) write:

> Every speaking, every voice, and thus every manifestation of the self is embedded in a specific discourse context, a context that on one hand makes the speaking possible but on the other hand shapes and limits what can be said in a particular situation.
>
> *(p. 640)*

In essence, every individual is embedded within a wider socio-cultural, historical, and political context that both shapes who we are and what we can say. Although conferring limitations on what we write, Sermijn et al.'s statement also situates the writer within a wider context – not isolated but engaged in society – legitimating their ability to write about their lived experiences, reflecting and mirroring life in general.

Autoethnography offers the possibility of including the often-marginalised voices of those on the fringes of research. It is, therefore, frequently employed by researchers who want to catalyse change through exposing the lived lives of those caught up in social injustices, for there is "a need to tell to further social justice" (Pelias, 2011, p. 661), to reveal what has been silenced or hidden. Working for social justice is an important touchstone for the autoethnographic student to bear in mind – particularly when challenged with adverse comments that deem autoethnographic research as narcissistic, bearing the burden of intersubjectivity.

The challenge of speaking out

Expressing practitioner experience is challenging and exposing and not something all practitioners will be comfortable with. Insight into the challenges facing practitioners was recognised by Connelly and Clandinin (1995), who commented that teachers' stories are more than just tales: they happen within a landscape that is essentially "moral" (p. 11). Nothing enters that is "value-neutral" (ibid). Such a context promotes certain ways of being, while other forms of behaviour may be seen as unacceptable. Perhaps this is why Connelly and Clandinin suggested that there was more to learn from teachers' tales – especially those to be told from behind the door, defined as secret stories that were embedded in "epistemological and moral dilemmas" (p. 14) within teachers' practices. These were the silenced stories, usually covered up, to evoke a sense of certainty and expertise instead of tension, the stories hidden in order to maintain a professional identity.

To that end, the work of Connelly and Clandinin exposes the challenge and moral dilemma facing practitioners who want to speak out, but are afraid of "being known" (Gingras, 2012, p. 80) and the exposure that might consequently label them as unfit for practice. The transparency generated through writing about 'self' might encourage others to pathologise or psychologise the vulnerabilities of writers, a risk that might be too high for some (Etherington, 2004). The risk of "exposing ourselves to censure or ridicule or marginalisation" through sharing our stories with others, is, as Ball (2015b, p. 13) reminds us, very real. With no guarantee of sensitive readership, writers must therefore negotiate the degree to which they want to expose themselves, while being mindful of future consequences for, ultimately, what is written goes beyond the writer's control, into the hands of readers. At a time of growing tensions within early years practice, leaving many practitioners simply playing a "game" (Basford and Bath, 2014, p. 122) to survive, is it safe for practitioners to speak out? Consider, however, what their inner stories might reveal about early years practice and what is lost in their absence. Aren't these stories worth listening to?

Caring for self and others

Research students today must comply with ethical approval protocols that give consideration of risk to self and others. Such processes strive to ensure that researchers uphold the rights of others while also taking into account their own safety and well-being; no one should be harmed as a consequence of any research process. Consideration for others is not new, however, and within the medical profession, the need to uphold a code of ethics, to ensure adopting practices that would not harm anyone, can be traced back to the swearing of the Hippocratic Oath in the fifth century BC (Anderson, 2004).

Obtaining ethical approval to carry out a study, however, does not absolve the researcher or writer of any further ethical considerations, for they are constantly changing, fluid, and in need of regular scrutiny as the research process unfolds and develops. Nevertheless, although prescriptive ethical codes are limited, they also stand as a reminder of the asymmetry of power in the research process through the researcher's knowledge of the 'other.' Relational ethics are therefore pertinent here, for the need to protect others involved in writing and research is paramount if researchers are to avert causing a disservice to "the very people (*research*) is meant to represent and address" (Goodley et al., 2004, p. 174, my italics).

Writing autoethnographic narratives invariably involves writing about self and others. Yet, keeping close to actual experiences, in order to maintain a feeling of verisimilitude in the stories, is not congruent with ethical codes to protect those involved in the research process. Conventionally, researchers and writers have traditionally employed tools such as changing the names and places of those involved to confer anonymity. In autoethnographic research, however, further considerations need to be applied in order to protect close friends and family members who may be implicated in the text too, transparently or tangentially, leading to an ethical tension that may not be resolved. To overcome this, Clough (2004a) suggests borrowing from real characters and fictionalizing them, melding characters from real events together to create a new character, thereby averting the possibility of identification. However, "The conscious theft of glimpses of people's lives in the interests of research" (Clough, 2004b, p. 376) is a moral dilemma, which, despite conferring anonymity, may still constitute a "betrayal" (p. 381) of those involved. This is amplified by Goodley (2004b) when he asks what right a researcher has to "forage for neat soundbites and distressing experiences" (p. 75) to produce a text.

In instances where I felt my narratives could be damaging either to the children, their families, or myself I applied an ethic of care (Ellis, 2009) and adopted Clough's (2002) fictionalizing technique, while remaining as faithful as possible to the core of the experience. Nevertheless, these are real and serious ethical dilemmas to which there is no prescriptive answer. Measured advice, however, is offered by Goodley (2004b) concerning the representation of others, when he suggests researchers "own(ed) the narratives in ways that highlight(ed) the human spirit" (p. 76) conferring dignity and respect. Adding to this are

Dauphinee's (2010, p. 818) words that "Responsibility, ethics, and love are not the same. But they often enable one another."

Children talking through silence

The publication in 1989 of the United Nations Charter on the Rights of the Child (UNCRC) meant a "radical shift in the status of children in society and in the structure of relationships between adults and children" (Lansdown, 1996, p. 9). The UNCRC (United Nations, 1989) conferred rights on children to adequate protection, participation, and provision in society. Within education in the Western world, this translated in part as the right for children to participate in decision making on matters that affected them. Concurrently, a discourse on 'listening' to children developed, informed in large part by discourse developed within the *Reggio Emilia* schools in Northern Italy promulgated by Dahlberg et al. (2007), which gave insight into new ways of observing children learning and including children in their learning. Consequent to these changes, educational researchers evolved and adopted new ways of including children in research based primarily on the Mosaic Approach developed by Clark and Moss (2001). This approach spawned a variety of ways of capturing children's views and 'voices' within research by encouraging children to participate.

It is important to note, however, that 'listening' in research and the use of child participatory methods is another hermeneutic process in which adults employ ethnographic tools with which to represent children's lives, such as photos or interviews of their time with children. Bath (2013) cautions that 'listening' needs to be "multimodal" (p. 363) in order to include those children who communicate in a variety of ways. While there is a growing body of research involving children directly in the research processes and the reporting of it (for example, see Gray and Winter, 2011), most research with children still involves adult translation and interpretation. Interpretation is complicated here by the fact that children are situated within an asymmetry of power with adults, located within spaces both constructed and controlled by the adults (Mannion, 2007), therefore ultimately impacting on what children feel they can say and subsequently what is then heard by the adults.

The stories I tell in this book, however, do *not* constitute child participatory research in which children drive the research or are engaged as equal partners with the researcher, but they do take place within the concept of everyday nursery 'listening' and 'child participation,' incumbent with its asymmetry of power. My 'listening' is born out of what Nutbrown (1996, p. 45) has called the "wide eyes and open minds (*with which to*) see clearly and to understand what (*children*) see" (my italics). Daily listening in work with young children attunes practitioners intimately with their children, coming to deeply know their ways. I concur with Nutbrown's call to observe children's learning sensitively when she says:

> Educators need wide eyes too, to guard against stereotypes and to combat prejudices about capabilities of children based on such factors as their gender, race, language, culture or disability.

> *(ibid)*

To the extent that my stories happen in the everyday practice of a nursery, they reflect the messiness of nursery life, the unresolved issues, the tensions, and the possibilities. It is imperative, however, not to mirror the weaknesses of the early ethnographers, echoing the "omniscient narrator" noted by Erikson (2011, p. 56) and therefore I have tried to be mindful of my representations and positioning of the children who were in my care. I am, however, aware that these real stories are recalled and written through my memory of the experiences we had, through my personal lens. I cannot therefore infer that I am representing the children in my stories, but rather they are an expression of my memory of them and as such are situated within temporal moments – events subject to changes in understanding and meaning over time. This is an intrinsic part of autoethnographic writing.

Self-care

With the re-emergence of the "bodily impact of the teacher-student relation" (Watkins, 2011, p. 137) during my writing, I became acutely aware of possible emotional injury to self. As part of an autoethnographic endeavour, emotional impact is unavoidable as the writer trawls through personal experiences and ploughs furrows through memoried events. Negotiating similar emotional upheaval in her research led Denshire (2014) to seek "opportunities to de-brief" (p. 841), yet she continues:

> Despite the challenge, discomfort and occasional joy of writing auto-ethnography, it is important to press on with the auto-ethnographic project in order to destabilize and redraw the boundaries between a professional's work and their life, creating space for dialogue with previously silenced others.
>
> *(p. 845)*

Like Denshire, I frequently needed to "de-brief" (p. 841) and am thankful to friends and family who shared their time with me. Similarly, concurring with Denshire, I agree with the view that autoethnographic labour is worthwhile, but the choice to write and what to write remains personal and individual.

Some critics see the "retreat into autoethnography (as) an abrogation of the honourable trade of the scholar" (Delamont, 2009, p. 61), stating that research should be concerned with social actors and their contexts, not "the introspection of the researcher" (p. 58) who is, after all, privileged and powerful (p. 59). The collection of data and introspection are not to be conflated, stresses Delamont, and research is not meant to be experiential but analytical. I put these thoughts here as they belong to an ethic of self-care in the sense that such overt criticism may be a factor in detracting from a writer's sense of self-worth or well-being. However, criticism of academic writing is nothing new and should, as a matter of course, be expected. It also needs to be weighed up in the context of the purpose of the research or writing, which in the case of autoethnography can be to generate a deeper understanding of "social life" (Sparkes, 2013, p. 177) and to help "implement a truly global social justice agenda" (Denzin, 2014b, p. 1,126). Autoethnography is helping to "speak back" (Denshire, 2014, p. 845) to audit cultures on behalf of marginalised and silenced voices, countering criticisms of those who see it as a form of "researcher self-obsession" (p. 844), but it has to make a difference to be worthwhile, to outweigh the risks.

Strength

As a methodology, autoethnography adds complexity to the well-trodden pathways of conventional research, breaching and blurring boundaries as it goes. Consequently, it attracts criticism on many different levels, one of which is the question of legitimacy; is it valid or not as research? The meaning of the word validity derives from the Latin word *validas,* which means "strong, powerful, and effective" (Polkinghorne, 2007, p. 474), suggesting that validity is relative, a matter of degree. How then might autoethnographic studies be judged, for the adoption and application of prescriptive and predetermined rules to research lead to a sense of governance over what is acceptable and legitimate (Sparkes, 2009), creating a dilemma for those engaged in non-conventional research and writing? Such rules, a throwback to positivist tendencies, are inscribed in the words of Lord Kelvin, who, in the 1800s declared that if something could not be measured in numbers, the consequent knowledge gained was meagre, worthless, and unscientific (in Conte and Dean, 2006, p. 59).

Several writers from within the autoethnographic community have suggested alternative ways of approaching the issue of validity, helping avoid an impasse and the notion that anything goes. The notion of "verisimilitude" (Ellis, 1999, p. 673), the ability of a text to speak to our own experiences, and connecting "heart to heart" (Pelias, 2004, p. 12) with readers are both proffered by several writers as tools for assessing the strength of an autoethnographic narrative. They do, however, assume active readership, and this may not always be guaranteed. It is also important to remember that while good writing will undoubtedly make connections with readers, the dilemmas experienced here are consequent to the positioning of autoethnography between art and science: As Hirshfield (2015) notes, theory belongs to argument; good writing belongs to art.

With further considerations of strength, Riessman (2008), in her work on narratives, foregrounds the importance of a text's usefulness and its ability to become the catalyst or foundation on which others base their work (p. 193); the strength of a text lies in its ability to effect change. Similarly, Sparkes (2013) foregrounds the importance of autoethnographic texts to deepen our understanding of the processes at work in society. A failure to work discursively, however, to provide frameworks for greater understanding, runs the risk of entrapment in "solipsistic self-misunderstanding" (Ploder and Stadlbauer, 2016, p. 756), leading critics to view this as weakening autoethnographers' claims of effecting social change. Such criticism positions autoethnography as weak, insubstantial, and dangerous and, as Ploder and Stadlbauer indicate, in German-speaking cultures, they have been warned off and discouraged from adopting autoethnography as a methodology. Holman Jones' (2016) response, however, is to promote critical autoethnography, which has the potential to overcome any perceived weakness through a lack of "theoretical frameworks" (p. 288).

Tolerance, however, is called for amongst the research community, to remain open to other ways of researching and writing, even within the ethnographic community itself (Sparkes, 2009: Denzin, 2014b), to avert stagnation within research. For at risk here is the loss of powerful stories such as Spry's (2011b) poetic performative paper on 'The accusing body' working with the experience of rape, Smith's (2013) shared poetic prose on depression and attempted suicide, or McCrea's (2014) shared self-narrative on becoming an adoptive parent, contextualised within the turbulence of politics in Guatemala. In turn, these stories draw the reader in, "implicating them" (Pelias, 2011, p. 667), to encourage action on behalf of social justice and to develop an empathy for the lived experiences of others. There are few ways to do this so powerfully.

10

ANALYSIS

Speaking and reading from the heart

Analysis: is it necessary?

When two-year-old children see a train, they frequently refer to it as a 'choo-choo.' Similarly, they often differentiate animals by the sounds they make, such as 'meow' for cat and 'woof-woof' for dog. Young children develop an inner relationship to objects in the world through their function (Vygotsky and Luria, 1994), going on to share their understanding of the world and its objects by imitating the sounds or actions of these objects rather than using the more abstract nouns used by adults. For children, the noun may be perceived as a whole range of actions and sounds captured or trapped inside one word, the verb effectively frozen by language. In my experience, young children relate more to the being-ness and function of an object than its abstract name. In Chapter 8, I noted Ingold's (2015) illustration of the Tlingit people of the northwest Pacific Coast and their relationship with glaciers, which they perceive as the living embodiment of "sound, light and feeling" (p. 82). This is not dissimilar to a child's inner perception of the world around them and leads me to suggest that adults may have lost their sensitivity for the meaning of words in our overly abstract, cognitive world. In other words, the relationship between the power of our words and our inner relationship to objects to affect us and hold deep meaning has diminished since childhood.

Traditionally, qualitative researchers have engaged with abstract activities involving coding and analysing data, mirroring the more positivist approach taken by the scientific community in their research. Everything has its place in research and coding and analysis are necessary tools with which to measure the efficacy of a medical intervention or obtain the demographics of a particular place or group of people in order to plan for services and resources. But what is relevant when the data in research is formed of self-narratives, of vibrant life experiences? How should that be analysed, if at all? And how might we avoid becoming reductive, effectively freezing the self-narrative life-story event into a word or code, losing its vibrancy and power to move hearts and minds?

Resisting habituated practices, including those in research, means stepping out of the known comfort zones of the research world to engage with risk, thereby re-defining what research might do and exploring what is possible. The well-travelled pathways of conventional research that call upon researchers to adopt prescribed formats, such as writing a literature review or analysing data, do not find a comfortable fit with the intentions of autoethnographic writing. This means that the autoethnographic researcher has to further embrace both challenge and opportunity.

Indicating that research design and writing up data need not follow prescribed routes Kamler and Thomson (2014) point out that literature, once written in a research text, is often then abandoned to the margins of research and little referred to within the body of the wider work. What often then follows leaves little room for readers to invoke their own meaning as the researcher usually goes on to code, analyse, and discuss their findings and conclusions. Autoethnography, on the other hand, seeks to light fires in research as opposed to filling buckets. While buckets have their place, we stand in need of fires to light the way forward, to shift paradigms in education. Perhaps autoethnography is re-enlivening our reductive and abstract world, thawing our nouns and our frozen verbs. Indeed, researchers previously dared not speak of emotion or personal experience in research, yet now there is a growing swell of research that draws the body "from the shadows of academe ... to interrogate it" as noted earlier by Spry (2001, p. 725).

Contesting analysis

The issue of analysis within autoethnographic research, an eclectic field of practices, is a contentious one. It should come as no surprise then to find that among autoethnographic scholars there exists, currently, a spectrum of opinion on the issue of analysis. Several writers contest the need for analysis by predetermined categories and coding (Ellis and Bochner, 2006; Pelias, 2011; St. Pierre, 2011), arguing that "writing is analysis" (St. Pierre, 2011, p. 621) and coding is adopted only because "we don't know how to teach thinking" (p. 622). Ellis and Bochner (2006), key proponents of autoethnography as a research methodology, hold that autoethnographic texts need to be understood as literature that seeks of itself to effect change, therefore any further analysis, for the sake of academic convention, simply detracts from the "qualities that make a story a story" (p. 440). But is unanalysed writing research?

The activity of writing itself filters the world through the lens of the writer, a personal analysis of life events. Pelias (2011) argues that "realizations ... unfold on a continuum from the personal to the public" (p. 660) through writing, enabling the writer to expose their values and beliefs. Writing openly and transparently situates the writer within a socio-cultural context relative to relevant discourses and is therefore open to analysis by the reader. Expressing the power of autoethnographic writing, Spry (2011a, p. 497) captures this in a poem, an extract of which follows:

Autoethnography is body and verse,
It is self and other and one and many.
It is ensemble, a cappella, and accompaniment.
Autoethnography is place and space and time,
It is personal, political, and palpable.

Autoethnographic writing speaks not only of the individual and their 'story' but socio-cultural and political values are simultaneously spoken through the story as the individual who speaks is embedded within a culture (Witherell and Noddings, 1991). The texts therefore expose the intersection between the personal and the political which, as Palmer (2007) reminds us, is where teaching always takes place – "at the crossroads of the personal and the public" (p. 66). Allowing the reader to develop their own perspective, through the multiple layers and voices of an autoethnographic narrative, is for many writers what this methodology is about.

Employing performative autoethnography has enabled me to create what Denzin (2006) refers to as a "chorus of discordant voices" (p. 433) to help readers locate my experiences within a socio-cultural context. I also chose to draw out key themes to further accentuate this which concurs with Langer's (2016) assertion that to pursue the "joint production of meaning" (p. 736) writers can open up a "dialogic space between the researcher, who tells his or her story, and the reader, who becomes a critical partner in the interpretation process" (p. 742). My own preference, to write beyond my autoethnographical narratives and into a discursive space, also signals my need, as a former practitioner, to offer further food for thought. This does not preclude the reader from making their own relationship to the narratives nor does it necessarily get in the way of letting the stories 'speak to the heart' (Pelias, 2004). Although I concur with Goodley (2004a) that "The beauty of emotions is that it so often works its way through a tide of repressive rational thought" (p. 177), and further concur with Pelias (2004) when he emphasises the need to "open a space of identification, a place of understanding ... to connect heart to heart" (p. 12), I also wanted to ensure that my reader was left in no doubt about the urgency and intensity of the issues in my stories. I therefore chose to contextualise each story so that they might do further "political work" (Riessman, 2008, p. 8). The reader is therefore free to further analyse the contextualised text through their own experiences and beyond.

Capturing this aspect of autoethnographic writing, Pelias (2011) states:

Personal utterances are revelatory in the public sphere ... and public pronouncement and legislation find their most profound articulation as they impact individual's bodies. By contemplating the personal, public realizations emerge; by considering the public, personal insights become apparent.

(p. 661)

The stories in this book are all about issues close to *my* heart and so, for this reason, the stories and the discursive spaces should now be left to speak to the *heart of the reader.* Further (personal) analysis will take place if a reader thinks "with" (Ellis, 2004, p. 197) my stories and considers the impact on them, for my perception of them is just that – and others will take (or leave) other things. "The proof for you is in the things I have made – how they look to your mind's eye, whether they satisfy your sense of style and craftsmanship, whether you believe them, and whether they appeal to your heart" (Sandelowski, 1994, p. 61).

11

ORIGINS

Sowing the seeds of personal values

'Somebody' haiku (ii)
In the awkward month
somebody's daughter is born
a full moon rises

(Thewless, 2009)

Once upon a time, the word *vocation* was frequently used to describe entering professions such as medicine, ministry, or education. Something inward is conveyed in this term, perhaps even more so in the term 'calling,' which was used interchangeably with the term 'vocation.' Such words are little used today and I sense that inwardness, for some reason, is seen as dangerous and unnecessary. Instead, in education today, our attention is drawn outwards – to career-paths, contracts, appraisal, inspections, regulations, and academic study. While I am not in any sense wanting to condemn or marginalise these aspects of our work, it leaves me wondering where the inner voice of the practitioner might find its place. Where might we speak of our vocation?

Teaching, at any level, is acknowledged as a stressful occupation, yet there is little regard for the need to pause and reflect, to be inward. Being outwardly busy has become the accepted norm of our time, while something of an institutional denial for the need to be inward has taken root. Perhaps that's why we need to write, to make sense of it all retrospectively? There is a recognised tendency in education to hide behind our professional role, within a profession that "fears the personal and seeks safety in the technical, the distant, the abstract" (Palmer, 2007, p. 12). When practitioners bow to pressure, however, they can feel a sense of disconnectedness within their practice, a feeling that it is both "inauthentic and alienating" (Ball, 2010, p. 126), leading to a lack of coherence, a schism, which in turn impacts on their long-term commitment to the profession. As Ball notes, our deeper values may be "sacrificed for impression" (ibid). Yet, young children have an incredible capacity to sense authenticity, integrity, or the lack of them in adults, leading Palmer (2007) to suggest that the "selfhood of the teacher is key" (p. 7) to success.

When Freire (1972) wrote about hope in education in the 1970s, he called upon us to name the world and ourselves – to know our own narratives in order to make choices, out of freedom. Self-knowledge is powerful and healing, leading to the possibility of self-determination. Autoethnography provides practitioners with a way of eliciting self-knowledge, looking inwards, backwards and then forwards, armed with insight. The writer bell hooks (1994) gives expression to something I have always felt about my work in education and care, namely its sacredness. Yet, I almost dare not to say it for fear of misinterpretation, for I don't mean something sacred in terms of religiousness but something sacred at the core of my being, your being, our being:

> To educate as the practice of freedom is a way of teaching that anyone can learn. That learning process comes easiest to those of us who teach who also believe that there is an aspect of our vocation that is sacred; who believe that our work is not merely to share information but to share in the intellectual and spiritual growth of our students. To teach in a manner that respects and cares for the souls of our students is essential if we are to provide the necessary conditions where learning can most deeply and intimately begin.
>
> *(hooks, 1994, p. 13)*

But, first of all we need to know ourselves, which Aristotle, in Ancient Greek times, believed was the beginning of all wisdom: 'Know thyself'. As hooks indicates, it is often necessary to "transgress those boundaries that would confine each pupil to a rote, assembly-line approach to learning" to achieve "mutual recognition" (ibid). Perhaps knowing ourselves helps to clarify our values and what is important in our interactions with the children in our care.

So, where does a practitioner's wayfaring line begin and what contributes to the development of such an identity? In her autoethnographic paper '*A box of childhood: small stories at the roots of a career*,' Nutbrown (2011) writes that she "always wanted to be a teacher" (p. 233) and could not remember a time when that wasn't the case. I share her sentiment and can remember announcing, at the age of five or six years old, to anyone who asked of me the question 'What do you want to do when you grow up?' that I would be a teacher. This often drew knowing smiles, a wink between the adults and frequent patting of their hands on my head (which I sensed was patronising) as they reflected on my life circumstances and the unlikely chance of success.

So, now I look back at my childhood to explore the roots of my career, my journey to working with young children, and its relationship to the stories in this book. These "ordinary fragments" (Nutbrown, 2011, p. 245) of my childhood, expressed here, have travelled with me throughout my career, both consciously and unconsciously. They have motivated, informed, and catalysed many of my professional actions and have found their expression within the stories earlier in this book: stories that centre on issues of difference, difficulty and marginalisation. I believe they find their origin in my childhood.

Marginalisation is painful. Children, through their teacher's attitudes and society's mores and values, can find themselves marginalised because of their race, ethnicity, faith, gender orientation, behaviour, disability... the list is endless. I was born on the cusp of a change, a shift in attitudes and understanding, that had not been fully adopted by everyone and I felt the full force of that. How easy it is to quash the fragile beginnings of a child's identity, their hopes and dreams, their ontological becomings.

Seeds

Oak trees and their largesse grow from little acorns, seeds sown both intentionally and unintentionally, by chance. Childhood is full of seeds, ontological seeds that can be nurtured or thwarted, especially by those who work with children or students.

* * *

When I was ten years old, I often walked into town on a Saturday morning to the public library to borrow the books I needed for my school project work. It was just over a mile and a pleasant walk at that. On arrival in town I first passed the police station, a glowing testament to poor architectural decision-making, based on utilitarian objectives in the early 1960s. Its matchbox-shaped outline jarred the eye and it reeked of fear and power in equal measure. I always cast my eyes ahead just at that point in my journey, perhaps out of an unconscious sense of fear, to look upwards to the church spire and the neighbouring red sandstone buildings that spoke of grandeur, mystery, and otherness.

In between the church, with its tolling bells and incense-filled vaporous air and the theatre on the opposite side of the road with its big oak doors, stood my library: a two-storey red sandstone building whose carved masonry exuded opulence and a pride in craftsmanship long gone. The interior held a dry, withered smell that I later came to associate with knowledge and academia; shelves stacked five or six storeys high and long oak tables, reminiscent of medieval banqueting times, overlooked by high cathedral-like ceilings, spoke to my senses. I took my place and sat down to embrace the stillness and quiet, conscientious ardour – and the mystery of knowledge – that permeated this place.

After an hour or so of intense reading and writing, I often wandered round the library, stopping to thumb through the big reference books that spoke of wonder-filled places and faraway people. I silently slipped between their pages, saturating my imagination with sensuous mysteries. Unbeknown to me then, I would one day travel to see many of them: the rainforests of northern Australia filled with deafening life; the majesty of the cold Tibetan plateau whose pure and unpolluted air exuded the fragrance of jasmine and roses; the warmth of the Mediterranean seas and the scent of rosemary, sage, and oregano carried on warm air; the golden gate of Jerusalem's city wall that remained firmly shut; the busy streets of Marrakesh, whose searing heat was punctuated with blaring car horns and Middle Eastern spices; the Great Wall of China, keeping insiders in and outsiders out; the Turkish tomb of Jelaluddin Rumi, whose Sufi poetry would one day save me from near-death and the incandescent colour-fuelled night wonder of the far north that we call the Aurora Borealis. I leaned into the strength and power of every page and dared to dream.

On taking up my seat once more, with intent and homework calling for completion, I lifted my pencil and began to write. After some time had passed, however, I had the disturbing feeling that I was being watched. I furtively glanced across the table to catch sight of an old man staring, somewhat open-mouthed, at me. I looked away and quickly centred my attention on the pages that lay in front of me on the table, my thoughts inflected by my mother's voice compelling me not to speak to strangers. I continued for a few moments before looking up again and wrinkling my forehead in disapproval in the direction of the elderly man, to ward him off. He jolted. I recoiled.

"Oh, my dear, I'm so sorry" he began, "I have interrupted your work and upset you." He paused.

I grimaced, deepening the wrinkles on my brow before retorting, somewhat defensively and abruptly, "Why are you staring at me?"

He sat back, and then looking straight at me, declared "I'm not staring at you. I'm looking at your hand and your writing. It is so beautiful".

I swiftly looked to both my writing and my hand then looked back at him, quizzically.

★ ★ ★

I set off for school at five years old with a hop, skip, and a jump and the promise of new things; my mum told me that I'd learn to read and write and do some sums. If I was good, she promised to let me start piano lessons and carry on with my skating lessons – that all seemed like a good deal to me. I quickly learned, however, that school would become a bewildering place for me, bringing pain and confusion into my life.

I was a bright child and embarrassingly eager to do well. I was competitive and wanted to learn quickly, so devoured knowledge with an insatiable appetite, perhaps due to the dearth of books in our house, which consisted of the Be-Ro Cookbook, the Hillman Imp car manual, a dictionary from Woolworth's made from cheap, browning paper priced 1/3d, a collection of poetry and songs by Robert Burns, Scotland's bard, and of course the standard volumes of *Encyclopaedia Britannica*, which lots of working-class children had in their homes if their parents were at all aspirational.

Our two-bedroom council house was very small, housing five people: my two brothers, mum, dad, and me. It was on the edge of an industrial estate hemmed in by a busy main road and railway lines to the north and south, connecting two major cities. Heavy industry pervaded our whole house as dad, who worked in the iron foundry and later at a steel metal factory that made buses, was joined by my older brother as an apprentice. Our house was always full of factory smells, grime, bits of buses, and talk of machines and trade union business, especially when we ate our tea at 5 o'clock.

We had a little back garden in which my dad grew lots of vegetables, which kept us going all summer and beyond. I had requested my own bit of it (two feet by three feet as I remember it) because I wanted to grow Livingstone daisies, which magically opened when the sun came out and closed when the clouds were in the sky or it rained, as it often did! They were like little fairies, I thought.

I knew all the local trees and their names; my favourite ones were the cherry trees on the roundabout near the end of our street that showered their blossoms onto our pavement and road in springtime. The pink petals made it look like a far-away land – it was so beautiful – yet my mum often said "Look at that mess all over the pavement!" and she would sweep the petals away. I loved dancing on them, pretending they could grant magic wishes like transporting me on a magic carpet of petals to places I'd read about.

We had lots of freedom to roam and often, with my friends, I bravely dodged big lorries as we crossed the main road, escaping to 'the other side' beyond the factories, to the wilderness. We gathered frog's spawn in jam jars and wildflowers for our mums and we 'larked about' getting really muddy and filthy. I was happy in my little bubble, with no real idea of how poor we were, nor what challenges lay ahead in my life as I went off to school on that first day with a hop, skip, and a jump and a real expectation of new things to come … and they did.

Mrs. Graham was a 'nice' teacher but very strict. On Friday afternoons, she asked us to close our eyes so that the fairies could come and leave us a sweetie for working so hard. But Mrs. Graham also brought confusion into my life when she smacked me in front of the class, lifting up my tartan kilt to skelp my bottom, while reminding me of my name and reprimanding me for helping my friend, John Thompson, to write the letter 'P' in his book. He struggled with his writing and I was good at 'P' so I wrote his for him. In fact, I did a whole page and Mrs. Graham was not pleased. I became very confused but got used to being hit for helping others.

In primary two, when I was six years old, we were introduced to joined-up writing and I got very muddled one day because I wrote my whole name backwards at the bottom right corner of the page, working my way from right to left while everybody else started at the top and went from left to right. I thought maybe I was getting chickenpox like Linda and Becky because I had a sore head and felt dizzy. But I couldn't see my writing when I wrote from left to right because I had the pencil in my left hand, I couldn't see where I was going and that made it difficult to join up the letters. When Mrs. Graham asked me what

I thought I was doing, I explained that I couldn't see where I was going on the paper so had to write this way, but all she said was, "Stop being so silly and do it properly." I got *very* confused because now my writing went downhill and looked messy.

One day, an old lady came into our class. She was wearing a strange hat with a long pin in it and Mrs. Graham told us her name was Mrs. Straw. She was our sewing teacher. She didn't smile. We all lined up and went into the room that led to the school stage, which doubled as a classroom when there were no performances or rehearsals on it. They just shut the big curtains to make it look like a room, but we knew it was really the stage. Mrs. Straw gave each of us a needle, one by one, a scrap of white cloth, and a piece of thread, which I remember was red. She showed us how to thread the needle and how to put the needle into the cloth so that it left a red trail behind in the white cloth "like this," and she showed us her cloth. I managed to thread my needle and pushed it into my cloth and set off pricking the cloth and then rescuing the needle with a fair degree of enthusiasm.

Having got two lines done before Mrs. Straw got round the class (there were thirty-two of us in the class so it took her a while), I was feeling quite pleased with myself for having got further than John McDonald, Linda, and Lorna. Mrs. Straw came up the row and then paused by my desk. I awaited her approval but something strange happened next: She asked me to get up and go to the front of the class. Usually we went to the front of the class to show something off to the others, but as she had told me to leave my sewing behind, I had a strange feeling in my tummy. She didn't sound pleased and she was pushing me along, digging her hand into my back.

Calling the class to attention, she asked everyone to put their sewing down and listen, so they all stopped sewing and looked up at me and Mrs. Straw. Then she announced loudly, "If anyone sees Elizabeth sewing with her left hand, tell me straight away! She is not to do it. Do you understand?" She was angry, her words were harsh, shrill, piercing and I felt ashamed, though I couldn't understand what I'd done wrong. I had stitched as fast as I could and it *was* a bit messy, but it wasn't that bad! My classmates, however, all meekly nodded and I felt a sense of betrayal *and* shame: She had asked them to 'clype' on me and we didn't 'clype.'

Mrs. Straw then proceeded to push me back to my desk, her hand thrust in between my shoulder-blades, shoving me along at speed, and propelling me into my seat while pressing heavily on my shoulders. She bent over and whispered into my ear, "Left-handed people are evil. Don't let me catch you sewing with your left hand again." She tapped my shoulder twice before moving away.

I was thoroughly confused and wanted to run away from school. I didn't understand the word 'evil' but felt it meant something really bad and that made me feel scared. I started to feel hot and dizzy and things got worse as I just couldn't get the fingers on my right hand to work properly. It was no use: My sewing looked truly messy. I sat quietly trying to figure out what to do, and then I devised a plan. I could sew under the table with my left hand while keeping an eye on Mrs. Straw, and then switch to my right when she came anywhere near my desk. Somehow I knew this was bad and I really shouldn't do that. I felt sick in my tummy. I was confused and the big 'stage' room felt like it was going to swallow me up. I just wanted to go home.

Later, I explained to my grandma, who looked after us when mum was at work, what had happened in the sewing lesson. She understood because she had been beaten at school for writing with her left hand. My dad got beaten on his left hand with a stick one day at school until his fingers bled. Then his teacher said, "Now if you write with your left hand I'll see the blood on the paper." So he wrote with his right hand. Even now though, as an adult, he worried about his writing and thought it looked untidy.

"But what about that word, grandma?" I suddenly asked anxiously.

Yes, it was very bad, she said but what did Mrs. Straw know about left-handed people like us?

> If you want to sew under the table with your left hand, just do that. If Mrs. Straw gets on at you again just tell me, and I'll go up to that school and give her a piece of my mind!

I felt safe and understood, but I didn't like school anymore; it was a confusing place and it was no place for small children. It made me feel sick, very sick, especially on Tuesdays, sewing day.

★ ★ ★

"Please don't be afraid," he continued, "but could I ask to see your writing close up? May I hold it? My eyes are not so good these days." He gestured, with wizened fingers, in the direction of my notebook. Hesitantly I picked it up, feeling somewhat embarrassed: I knew my writing had been hurried and was therefore not my best. Slowly I handed over my book, watching his face all the while for signs. Then, I sloped back in my chair, expectantly. Would he admonish me? As I waited quietly and nervously, something of an 'other-worldly' feeling pervaded the air. It crept over me as he pondered the pages phlegmatically then gently smiled. Leaning over the table, he began to whisper with a hint of a Hebridean accent,

> My name is Michael John MacKendrick. I am eighty-two years old. I watched you writing with such confidence, my dear, that you brought a tear to my eye. Please forgive my intrusion but I am left-handed too, just like you, but I wasn't allowed to write with my left hand at school. I was beaten and punished and forced to write with my right hand. Do they allow it now in school? Or have you been punished too?

I stretched over the table and began to whisper the story of Mrs. Straw to him, followed by my grandmother's encouraging words. I told him that I was going to teach young children to make sure they got to write with their chosen hand and I would ensure they were not punished.

After some time, I began to wonder where we were, for it seemed possible that we had floated through the walls to the church next door, or perhaps we had talked our way through a time-veil? His dark soft eyes, freckled face and unassuming voice had beguiled me. Then, all of a sudden, a smile broke across my face as I realised he could see me. He could see me for who I am. Called out as 'evil' at six years old by an ignorant teacher, I now leaned in for comfort and healing at ten to the words of Michael John MacKendrick. "Be proud of who you are, my dear. Just *be* yourself and you will be alright.' Pushing himself into an upright position, slowly, he continued, 'And now I must let you get on with your work. I have taken up enough of your time. Goodbye now and thank you". He handed back my notebook. I thanked him and nodded. We smiled.

A few moments later, after pondering what had happened, I realised that I actually had lots of questions, so I turned around expectantly, hoping to catch a glimpse of Michael John MacKendrick. He was gone.

★ ★ ★

"Hope and education … share the same ontological root".

(Webb, 2010, p. 327 after Freire)

"The heart learns that stories are the truths that won't keep still".

(Pelias, 2004, p. 171)

REFERENCES

Aasen, W., Grindheim, L.T. and Waters, J. (2009). The outdoor environment as a site for children's participation, meaning-making and democratic learning: Examples from Norwegian kindergartens. *Education 3–13: International Journal of Primary, Elementary and Early Years Education*, 37, 1, 5–13. doi:10.1080/03004270802291749.

Adami, R. (2015). Re-thinking relations in human rights education: The politics of narratives. In M. Griffiths, M.H. Hoveid, S. Todd and C. Winter (Eds.) *Re-imagining relationships in education: Ethics, politics and practices* (pp. 126–142). West Sussex, United Kingdom: Wiley Blackwell.

Adams, P. (2015). In defence of care: Gilligan's relevance for primary education. *Pedagogy, Culture & Society*, 23, 2, 281–300. doi:10.1080/14681366.2014.994662.

Ahmed, S. (2004). *The cultural politics of emotion*. Edinburgh, Scotland: Edinburgh University Press.

Altheide, D.L. and Johnson, J.M. (2011). Reflections on interpretive adequacy in qualitative research. In N.K. Denzin and Y.S. Lincoln (Eds.) *The SAGE handbook of qualitative research* (4th ed.) (pp. 581–594). London, England: SAGE.

Anderson, L. (2006). Analytic autoethnography. *Journal of Contemporary Ethnography*, 35, 4, 373–395. doi:10.1177/0891241605280449.

Anderson, P. (2004). Ethics. In S. Fraser, V. Lewis, S. Ding, M. Kellett and C. Robinson (Eds.) *Doing research with children and young people*. (pp. 97–111). London, England: SAGE Publications Ltd.

Antonovsky, A. (1993). Complexity, conflict, chaos, coherence, coercion and civility. *Social Science and Medicine*, 37, 8, 969–981.

Ball, S.J. (2003). The teacher's soul and the terrors of performativity. *Journal of Education Policy*, 18, 2, 215–228. doi:10.1080/0268093022000043065.

Ball, S.J. (2010). New voices, new knowledge and the new politics of education research: The gathering of a perfect storm? *European Educational Research Journal*, 9, 2, 124–137. doi:10.2304/eerj.2010.9.2.124.

Ball, S.J. (2015a). Education, governance and the tyranny of numbers. *Journal of Education Policy*, 30, 3, 299–301. doi:10.1080/02680939.2015.1013271.

Ball, S.J. (2015b). Subjectivity as a site of struggle: Refusing neoliberalism? *British Journal of Sociology of Education*. doi:10.1080/01/01425692.2015.1044072; http://dx.doi.org/10.1080/01425692.2015.1044072.

Balogh, R. (2010). 'In dreams begins responsibility': A self-study about how insights from dreams may be brought into the sphere of action research. *Educational Action Research*, 18, 4, 517–529. doi:10.1080/09650792.2010.524829.

Banting, K. (1985). Poverty and educational priority. In I. McNay and J. Ozga (Eds.) *Policy-making in education* (pp. 291–313). Oxford, England: Pergamon Press.

Barnardos (2016). Children affected by parental imprisonment. Retrieved April 2016 from www.barnardos.org.uk/what_we_do/our_work/children_of_prisoners.htm.

Barraclough, S.J. (2014). Migration of identity of a counsellor educator: Using writing as a method of inquiry to explore the in-between spaces. *Reflexive Practice: International and Multidisciplinary Perspectives*, 15, 3, 363–377. doi:10.1080/14623943.2014.900013.

Bartos, A.E. (2013). Children sensing place. *Emotion, Space and Society*, 9, 89–98. doi:10.1016/j.emospa.2013.02.008.

Basford, J. and Bath, C. (2014). Playing the assessment game: An English early childhood perspective. *Early Years: An International Research Journal*, 34, 2, 119–132. doi:10.1080/09575146.2014.903386.

Batchelor, D. (2012). Borderline space for voice. *International Journal of Inclusive Education*, 16, 5–6, 597–608. doi:10.1080/13603116.2012.655501.

Bath, C. (2013). Conceptualising listening to young children as an ethic of care in early childhood education and care. *Children and Society*, 27, 361–371. doi:10.1111/j.1099-0860.2011.00407.x.

Beauchamp, C. and Thomas, L. (2009). Understanding teacher identity: An overview of issues in the literature and implications for teacher education. *Cambridge Journal of Education*, 39, 2, 175–189. doi:10.1080/03057640902902252.

Belgutay, J. (2015, May 22). "Poverty is 'no excuse' for poor attainment": Education minister calls for 'honest evaluation' of system failings. *Times Education Supplement Scotland*, No. 2420, 6–7.

Bentley, H., O'Hagan, O., Brown, A., Vasco, N., Lynch, C., Peppiate, J., Webber, M., Ball, R., Miller, P., Byrne, A., Hafizi, M., and Letendrie, F. (2017). *How safe are our children?: the most comprehensive overview of child protection in the UK*. NSPCC, England. Retrieved July 21, 2017 from: https://www.nspcc.org.uk/globalassets/documents/research-reports/how-safe-children-2017-report.pdf.

Bertram, T. and Pascal, C. (2002). *The OECD thematic review of early childhood education and care: Background report for the United Kingdom*. Retrieved December 10, 2007 from www.oecd.org/dataoecd/48/16/2479205.

Blanchet-Cohen, N. and Elliot, E. (2011). Young children and educators engagement and learning outdoors: A basis for rights-based programming. *Early Education & Development*, 22, 5, 757–777. doi:10.1080/10409289.2011.596460.

Bourdieu, P. (1986). The forms of capital. In J.G. Richardson (Ed.) *Handbook of theory and research for the sociology of education* (pp. 241–258). London, England: Greenwood Press, Inc.

Bradshaw, P. and Tipping, S. (2010). *Growing up in Scotland: Children's social, emotional and behavioural characteristics at entry to primary school*. Edinburgh, Scotland: Scottish Government. Retrieved January 17, 2015 from www.gov.scot/Resource/Doc/310461/0097972.pdf.

Brogden, L.M. (2008). art·I/f/act·ology: curricular artifacts in autoethnographic research. *Qualitative Inquiry*, 14, 851–864. doi:10.1177/1077800408318301.

Brogden, L.M. (2010). Identities (Academic + Private) = Subjectivities (desire): Re: collecting art·I/f/acts. *Qualitative Inquiry*, 16, 368–377. doi:10.1177/1077800410364354.

Brooker, L. (2002). *Starting school: Young children learning cultures*. Berkshire, England: Open University Press.

Care Inspectorate (2016). *My World Outdoors: sharing good practice in how early years services can provide play and learning wholly or partially outdoors*. Dundee, Scotland: Care Inspectorate. Retrieved September 3, 2016 from: http://www.careinspectorate. com/images/documents/3091/My_world_outdoors_-_early_years_good_practice_ 2016.pdf.

Chang, H.V. (2009). *Autoethnography as method (developing qualitative inquiry)*. London, England: Routledge.

Child Poverty Action Group (2015). *Child poverty facts and figures*. Retrieved July 2, 2015 from www.cpag.org.uk/child-poverty-facts-and-figures.

Chopra, D. and Tanzi, R.E. (2012). *Super brain: Unleashing the explosive power of your mind to maximize health, happiness, and spiritual well-being*. London, England: Rider.

Chowdry, H. and Oppenheim, C. (2015). *Spending on late intervention: How can we do better for less*. Retrieved August 11, 2015 from www.eif.org.uk/wp-contents/ uploads/2015/02/SPENDING-ON-LATE-INTERVENTION.PDF.

Clandinin, D.J. and Connelly, F.M. (2000). *Narrative inquiry: Experience and story in qualitative research*. San Francisco, United States: Wiley.

Clandinin, D.J., Schaefer, L. and Downey, C.A. (Eds.) (2014). *Narrative conceptions of knowledge: Towards understanding teacher attrition*. Bingley, England: Emerald Group Publishing Ltd. Retrieved April 24, 2015 from http://dx.doi.org/10.1108/S1479-368720140000023000.

Clark, A. and Moss, P. (2001). *Listening to young children: The Mosaic approach*. London, England: National Children's Bureau Enterprises Ltd.

Claxton, G. (1999). *Wise up: Learning to live the learning life*. Stafford, England: Network Educational Press Ltd.

Clough, P. (2002). *Narratives and fictions in educational research*. Buckingham, England: Open University Press.

Clough, P. (2004a). Approaching: methodology in life story research: A non-participatory fiction. In D. Goodley, R. Lawthom, P. Clough and M. Moore (Eds.) *Researching life stories: Method, theory and analyses in a biographical age* (pp. 66–69). London, England: RoutledgeFalmer.

Clough, P. (2004b). Theft and ethics in life portrayal: Lolly — the final story. *International Journal of Qualitative Studies in Education*, 17, 3, 371–382. doi:10.1080/09518390 42000204642.

Connelly, F.M. and Clandinin, D.J. (1995). Teachers' professional knowledge landscapes: Secret, sacred, and cover stories. In D.J. Clandinin and F.M. Connelly (Eds.) *Teachers' professional knowledge landscapes* (pp. 3–15). London, England: Teachers College Press.

Conroy, J.C. (2004). *Betwixt and between: The liminal imagination, education and democracy*. Oxford, England: Peter Lang.

Conte, J.M. and Dean, M.A. (2006). Can emotional intelligence be measured? In K.R. Murphy (Ed.) *A critique of emotional intelligence: What are the problems and how can they be fixed?* (pp. 59–78). London, England: Erlbaum Associates.

Cottle, M. and Alexander, E. (2014). Parent partnership and 'quality' early years services: Practitioners' perspectives. *European Early Childhood Education Research Journal*, 22, 5, 637–659. doi:10.1080/1350293X.2013.788314.

CPAG (2017). *Child Poverty Facts and Figures*. Retrieved July 22, 2017 from: http://www. cpag.org.uk/child-poverty-facts-and-figures.

Crotty, M. (1998). *The foundations of social research: Meaning and perspective in the research process*. London, England: SAGE.

Csikszentmihalyi, M. (1991). *Flow: The psychology of optimal experience*. New York, United States: Harper Perennial.

Dahlberg, G., Moss, P. and Pence, A. (2007). *Beyond quality in early childhood education and care: Languages of evaluation* (2nd ed.). London, England: Routledge.

Damasio, A. (2000). *The feeling of what happens: Body, emotion and the making of consciousness.* London, England: Vintage Books.

Dauphinee, E. (2010). The ethics of autoethnography. *Review of International Studies*, 36, 3, 799–818. doi:10.1017/S0260210510000690.

Davies, B. (2011). Open listening: Creative evolution in early childhood settings. OMEP XXVI World Conference, August 11–13, 2010, Gothenburg, Sweden. *International Journal of Early Childhood*, 43, 119–132. doi:10.1007/s13158-011-0030-1.

Delamont, S. (2009). The only honest thing: Autoethnography, reflexivity and small crises in fieldwork. *Ethnography and Education*, 4, 1, 51–63. doi:10.1080/17457820802703507.

Deleuze, G. and Guattari, F. (1987, 2013). *A thousand plateaus: Capitalism and schizophrenia* (Trans. B. Massumi). London, England: Bloomsbury Publishing Plc.

Denshire, S. (2014). On autoethnography. *Current Sociology Review*, 62, 6, 831–850. doi:10.1177/0011392114533339.

Denzin, N.K. (1989). *Interpretive biography.* London, England: SAGE Publications.

Denzin, N.K. (2006). Analytic autoethnography, or déjà vu all over again. *Journal of Contemporary Ethnography*, 35, 4, 419–428. doi:10.1177/0891241606286985.

Denzin, N.K. (2014a). *Interpretive autoethnography* (2nd ed.). London, England: SAGE Publications Inc.

Denzin, N.K. (2014b). Reading the challenges of a global community and the sociological imagination. *Qualitative Inquiry*, 20, 9, 1122–1127. doi:10.1177/1077800414542934.

Denzin, N.K. and Lincoln, Y.S. (2011a). Introduction: The discipline and practice of qualitative research. In N.K. Denzin and Y.S. Lincoln (Eds.) *The SAGE handbook of qualitative research* (4th ed.) (pp. 1–19). London, England: SAGE.

Denzin, N.K. and Lincoln, Y.S. (2011b). Preface. In N.K. Denzin and Y.S. Lincoln (Eds.) *The SAGE handbook of qualitative research* (4th ed.) (pp. ix–xvi). London, England: SAGE.

Downey, C.A., Schaefer, L. and Clandinin, D.J. (2014). Composing a life in two knowledge landscapes. In D.J. Clandinin, L. Schaefer and C.A. Downey (Eds.) (2014). *Narrative conceptions of knowledge-towards understanding teacher attrition* (pp. 179–197). Bingley, England: Emerald Group Publishing Ltd. Retrieved April 24, 2015 from http://dx.doi.org/10.1108/S1479-368720140000023008.

Ecclestone, K. and Brunila, K. (2015). Governing emotionally vulnerable subjects and 'therapisation' of social justice. *Pedagogy, Culture & Society*, 23, 4, 485–506. doi:10.1080/14681366.2015.1015152.

Ecclestone, K. and Hayes, D. (2009). *The dangerous rise of therapeutic education.* Oxon, England: Routledge.

Ecclestone, K. and Lewis, L. (2014). Interventions for resilience in educational settings: Challenging policy discourses of risk and vulnerability. *Journal of Education Policy*, 29, 2, 195–216. doi:10.1080/02680939.2013.806678.

Education Scotland and Glasgow City Council (2017). Applying Nurture as a Whole School Approach: A Framework to support the Self-Evaluation of Nurturing Approaches in Schools and Early Learning and Childcare (ELC) Settings. Livingston, Scotland: Education Scotland. Retrieved June 16, 2017 from: https://education.gov.scot/improvement/Documents/inc55ApplyingNurturingApproaches.pdf.

Elfer, P. and Dearnley, K. (2007). Nurseries and emotional well-being: Evaluating an emotionally containing model of professional development. *Early Years*, 27, 3, 267–279. doi:10.1080/09575140701594418.

Elliot, T.S. (1989). *Four quartets.* Reading, England: Faber and Faber.

Ellis, C. (1999). Heartful autoethnography. *Qualitative Health Research*, 9, 669–683. doi:10.1177/104973299129122153.

Ellis, C. (2004). *The ethnographic I: A methodological novel about autoethnography*. Oxford, England: Altamira Press.

Ellis, C. (2009). *Revision: Autoethnographic reflections on life and work*. Walnut Creek, United States: Left Coast Press Inc.

Ellis, C.S. and Bochner, A.P. (2006). Analyzing analytic autoethnography: An autopsy. *Journal of Contemporary Ethnography*, 35, 4, 429–449. doi:10.1177/0891241606286979.

End Child Poverty (2016). *Child poverty map of the UK*. Retrieved July 21, 2017 from: http://www.endchildpoverty.org.uk/poverty-in-your-area-2016/.

Erikson, F. (2011). A history of qualitative inquiry in social and educational research. In N.K. Denzin and Y.S. Lincoln (Eds.) *The SAGE handbook of qualitative research* (4th ed.) (pp. 43–60). London, England: SAGE.

Estyn (2014). *Tackling deprivation and raising standards: Pupil deprivation*. Wales: HMIe. Retrieved June 10, 2015 from www.estyn.gov.uk/english/docViewer/309390.0/pupil-deprivation-may-2014/?navmap=30,163.

Etherington, K. (2004). *Becoming a reflexive researcher: Using ourselves in research*. London, England: Jessica Kingsley Publisher.

Fielding, M. (2007). Beyond "voice": new roles, relations, and contexts in researching with young people. *Discourse: Studies in the Cultural Politics of Education*, 28, 3, 301–310. doi:10.1080/01596300701458780.

Fjørtoft, I. (2001). The natural environment as a playground for children: The impact of outdoor play activities in pre-primary schoolchildren. *Early Childhood Education Journal*, 29, 2, 111–117.

Flyvbjerg, B. (2001). *Making social science matter: Why social science inquiry fails and how it can succeed again* (Trans. Sampson, S.) Cambridge, England: Cambridge University Press.

Fook, J. (2014). Learning from and researching (my own) experience: A critical reflection on the experience of social difference. In S.L. Witkin (Ed.) *Narrating social work through autoethnography*. (pp. 120–140). New York, United States: Columbia University Press.

Forrester, G. (2005). All in a day's work: primary teachers 'performing' and 'caring'. *Gender and Education,* 17, 3, 271–287. doi:10.1080/09540250500145114.

Freire, P. (1972). *Pedagogy of the oppressed* (Trans. Ramos, M.B.). Middlesex, England: Penguin Education.

Furedi, F. (2006). *Culture of fear revisited: Risk taking and the morality of low expectation* (4th ed.). London, England: Continuum.

Gallagher, S. (2005). *How the body shapes the mind*. Oxford, England: Clarendon Press.

Galligan, A.C. (2000). That place where we live: The discovery of self through the creative play experience. *Journal of Child and Adolescent Psychiatric Nursing*, 13, 4, 169–176.

Garner, R. (2015, March 31). Nearly four in ten qualifying teachers quitting the classroom after one year. *Independent*. Retrieved from www.independent.co.uk/news/education/education-news/nearly-four-in-ten-qualifying-teachers-quitting-the-classroom-after-one-year.

Geddes, R., Frank, J. and Haw, S. (2011). A rapid review of key strategies to improve the cognitive and social development of children in Scotland. *Health Policy*, 101, 20–28. doi:10.1016/j.healthpol.2010.08.013.

Gerhardt, S. (2004). *Why love matters: How affection shapes a baby's brain*. London, England: Routledge.

Gibson, J.J. (1986). *The ecological approach to visual perception*. East Sussex, England: Psychology Press, Taylor and Francis Group.

Gill, S. (2014). Mapping the field of critical narrative. In I. Goodson and S. Gill (Eds.) *Critical narrative as pedagogy* (pp. 13–37). London, England: Bloomsbury.

Gillies, V. (2011). Social and emotional pedagogies: Critiquing the new orthodoxy of emotion in classroom behaviour management. *British Journal of Sociology of Education,* 32, 2, 185–202. doi:10.1080/01425692.2011.547305.

Gilligan, C. (1982, 1993). *In a different voice: Psychological theory and women's development.* London, England: Harvard University Press.

Gilligan, C. (1995). Hearing the difference: Theorizing connection. *Hypatia,* 10, 2, 120–127. www.jstor.org/stable/3810283.

Gingras, J. (2012). Embracing vulnerability: Completing the autofictive circle in health profession education. *Journal of Transformative Education,* 10, 67–89. doi:10.1177/1545968312460632.

Giroux, H.A. (2002). Educated hope in an age of privatized vision. *Cultural Studies↔Critical Methodologies,* 2, 1, 93–112.

Gitlin, A. and Myers, B. (1993). Beth's story: The search for the mother/teacher. In D. McLaughlin and W.G. Tierney (Eds.) *Naming silenced lives: Personal narratives and processes of educational change* (pp. 51–69). London, England: Routledge.

Goldstein, L.S. (1998). More than gentle smiles and warm hugs: Applying the ethic of care to early childhood education. *Journal of Research in Education,* 12, 2, 244–261.

Goldstein, L.S. (1999). The relational zone: The role of caring relationships in the co-construction of mind. *American Educational Research Journal,* 36, 3, 647–673. www.jstor.org/stable/1163553.

Goleman, D. (1996). *Emotional Intelligence: Why it matters more than IQ.* London, England: Bloomsbury.

Goodley, D. (2004a). A/Effecting: audience and effects in researching life stories: "Is it really like that?" Towards enlightening stories. In D. Goodley, R. Lawthom, P. Clough and M. Moore (Eds.) *Researching life stories: Method, theory and analyses in a biographical age* (pp. 175–178). London, England: RoutledgeFalmer.

Goodley, D. (2004b). Doing: Method in life story research: Ethics with Gerry O'Toole. In D. Goodley, R. Lawthom, P. Clough and M. Moore (Eds.) *Researching life stories: Method, theory and analyses in a biographical age* (pp. 75–76). London, England: RoutledgeFalmer.

Goodley, D. (2014). *Dis/ability studies: Theorising disablism and ableism.* London, England: Routledge.

Goodley, D., Lawthom, R., Clough, P. and Moore, M. (2004). Teaching: Craft and ethics in researching life stories. In D. Goodley, R. Lawthom, P. Clough and M. Moore (Eds.) *Researching life stories: Method, theory and analyses in a biographical age* (pp. 165–174). London, England: RoutledgeFalmer.

Goodson, I. (2014). Defining the self through autobiographical memory. In I. Goodson and S. Gill (Eds.) *Critical narrative as pedagogy* (pp. 123–146). London, England: Bloomsbury.

Goouch, K. (2009). Forging and fostering relationships in play: Whose zone is it anyway? In T. Papatheodorou and J. Moyles (Eds.) *Learning together in the early years: Exploring relational pedagogy* (pp. 139–151). London, England: Routledge.

Goouch, K. (2010). *Towards excellence in early years education: Exploring narratives of experience.* London. England: Routledge.

Gray, C. and Winter, E. (2011). Hearing voices: Participatory research with preschool children with and without disabilities. *European Early Childhood Research Journal,* 19, 3, 309–320. doi:10.1080/1350293X.2011.597963.

Hale-Jinks, C., Knopf, H. and Knopf, H. (2006). Tackling teacher turnover in childcare: Understanding causes and consequences, identifying solutions. *Childcare Education*, 82, 4, 219–226. doi:10.1080/00094056.2006.10522826.

Hammera, J. (2011). Performance autoethnography. In N.K. Denzin and Y.S. Lincoln (Eds.) *The SAGE handbook of qualitative research* (4th ed.) (pp. 317–329). London, England: SAGE.

Hargreaves, A. (2000). Mixed emotions: Teacher's perceptions of their interactions with students. *Teaching and Teacher Education*, 16, 811–826. www/Elsevier.com/locate/tate.

Hass, R. (2013). *The essential haiku: Versions of Bashō, Buson and Issa* (Trans. R. Hass). Northumberland, England: Bloodaxe Books.

Heckman, J.J., Moon, S.H., Pinto, R., Savelyev, P. and Yavitz, A. (2010). A new cost-benefit and rate of return analysis for the Perry Preschool Programme. *IZA Policy Paper 17*. Retrieved January 5, 2013 from http://ftp.iza.org/pp17.pdf.

Hickey-Moody, A. (2013). Affect as method: Feelings, aesthetics and affective pedagogy. In R. Coleman and J. Ringrose (Eds.) *Deleuze and research methodologies* (pp. 79–95). Edinburgh, Scotland: Edinburgh University Press.

Hirshfield, J. (2012). *Come, thief.* Northumberland, England: Bloodaxe Books Ltd.

Hirshfield, J. (2015). *Ten windows: How great poems transformed the world.* New York, United States: Alfred A. Knopf.

HMIE (2006). *Missing out: A report on children at risk of missing out on educational opportunities.* Retrieved January 6, 2013 from www.educationscotland.gov.uk/inspection andreview/Images/hmiemoeo_tcm4-712759.pdf.

Hobbs, L. (2012). Examining the aesthetic dimensions of teaching: Relationships between teacher knowledge, identity and passion. *Teaching and Teacher Education*, 28, 718–727. doi:10.1016/j.tate.2012.01.010.

Hochschild (2012). *The managed heart: Commercialization of human feeling* (2nd ed.). London, England: University of California Press Ltd.

Holman Jones, S. (2016). Living bodies of thought: The "critical" in critical autoethnography. *Qualitative Inquiry*, 22, 4, 228–237. doi:10.1177/1077800415622509.

hooks, B. (1994). *Teaching to transgress: Education as the practice of freedom.* London, England: Routledge.

Hope, G., Austin, R., Dismore, H., Hammond, S. and Whyte, T. (2007). Wild woods or urban jungle: Playing it safe or freedom to roam. *Education 3–13: International Journal of Primary, Elementary and Early Years Education*, 35, 4, 321–332. doi:10.1080/03004270701602442.

Hoveid, M.H. and Finne, A. (2015). 'You have to give of yourself': Care and love on pedagogical relations. In M. Griffiths, M.H. Hoveid, S. Todd and C. Winter (Eds.) *Re-imagining relationships in education: Ethics, politics and practices* (pp. 73–88). West Sussex, United Kingdom: Wiley Blackwell.

Hudson, L. (1967). *Contrary imaginations: A psychological study of the English schoolboy.* Middlesex, England: Penguin.

Hydén, L.-C. (2013). Bodies, embodiment and stories. In M. Andrews, C. Squire and M. Tamboukou (Eds.) *Doing narrative research* (2nd ed.) (pp. 126–141). London, England: SAGE Publications Ltd.

Ingold, T. (2007). *Lines: A brief history.* London, England: Routledge.

Ingold, T. (2015). *The life of lines.* London, England: Routledge.

Ipsos MORI and Nairn, A. (2011). *Children's well-being in UK, Sweden and Spain: The role of inequality and materialism.* Retrieved October 10, 2014 from https://downloads.unicef.org.uk/wp-content/uploads/2011/09/IPSOS_UNICEF_ChildWellBeingreport.pdf?_ga=2.78912467.659137854.1497786389-558619847.1497786389.

Isenbarger, L. and Zembylas, M. (2006). The emotional labour of caring in teaching. *Teaching and Teacher Education,* 22, 120–134. doi:10.1016/jtate.2005.07.002.

Jackson, A.Y. and Mazzei, L.A. (2008). Experience and "I" in autoethnography: A deconstruction. *International Review of Qualitative Research,* 1, 3, 299–318. www.jstor.org/stable/10.1525/irqr.2008.1.3.299.

James, A., Jenks, C. and Prout, A. (1998). *Theorizing childhood.* Cambridge, England: Polity Press.

Jenkins, N. (2011). Age and youth. In N. Jenkins, K. Jones and L. Rees (Eds.). *Another country: haiku poetry from Wales* (p. 53). Llandysul, Wales: Gwasg Gomer.

Jensen, A.S. (2014). The deluge. *European Early Childhood Education Research Journal,* 22, 1, 77–90. doi:10.1080/1350293X2013.865358.

Jensen, S.A., Broström, S. and Hansen, O.H. (2010). Critical perspectives on Danish early childhood education and care: Between the technical and the political. *Early Years: An International Research Journal,* 30, 3, 243–254. doi:10.1080/09575146.2010.506599.

Joyce, R. (2012). *Outdoor learning: Past and present.* Berkshire, England: Open University Press.

Jütte, S., Bentley, H., Tallis, D., Mayes, J., Jetha, N., O'Hagan, O., Brookes, H. and McConnell, N. (2016). *How safe are our children?: the most comprehensive overview of child protection in the UK.* NSPCC, England. Retrieved July 22, 2017 from: https://www.nspcc.org.uk/globalassets/documents/research-reports/how-safe-children-2015-report.pdf.

Kamler, B. and Thomson, P. (2014). *Helping doctoral students write: Pedagogies for supervision* (2nd ed.). London, England: Routledge.

Kellmer Pringle, M. (1975). *The needs of children.* London, England: Hutchinson & Co (Publishers) Ltd.

Kenway, P., Bushe, S., Tinson, A. and Born, T.B. (2015). *Monitoring poverty and social exclusion in Scotland 2015.* Retrieved August 2, 2015 from www.jrf.org.uk/sites/files/jrf/MPSE-scotland-full.pdf.

Kenway, J. and Youdell, D. (2011). The emotional geographies of education: Beginning a conversation. *Emotion, Space and Society,* 4, 131–136. doi:10.1016/j.emospa.2011.07.001.

Kidner, C. (2011). *SPICe Briefing; early years-subject profile: 11/51.* Edinburgh, Scotland: Scottish Parliament Information Centre. www.scottish.parliament.uk/Research BriefingsAndFactsheets/S4/SB_11-51.pdf.

King, J.R. (1998). *Uncommon caring: Learning from men who teach young children.* London, England: Teachers College Press.

Kirtsoglou, E. (2010). Dreaming the self: A unified approach towards dreams, subjectivity and the radical imagination. *History and Anthropology,* 21, 3, 321–335. doi:10.1080/02757206.2010.499908.

Kondo, D.K. (1990). *Crafting selves: Power, gender, and discourse of identity in a Japanese workplace.* London, England: The University of Chicago Press.

Kyriacou, C. (1987). Teacher stress and burnout: An international review. *Educational Research,* 29, 2, 146–152. doi:10/1080/0013188870290207.

Langer, P.C. (2016). The research vignette: Reflexive representation of qualitative inquiry – a methodological proposition. *Qualitative Inquiry,* 22, 9, 735–744. doi:10.1177/1077800416658066.

Lansdown, G. (1996). The United Nations Convention on the Rights of the Child: Progress in the United Kingdom. In C. Nutbrown (Ed.) *Respectful educators-capable learners: Children's rights and early education* (pp. 1–10). London, England: Paul Chapman Publishing Limited.

Lansdown, G. (2001). *Every child's right to be heard: A resource guide on the UN committee on the rights of the child. General comment no. 12.* London, England: Save the Children/UNICEF. www.savethechildren.org.uk/sites/default/files/docs/Every-Childs-Right-to-be-Heard_0.pdf.

Lasky, S. (2005). A sociocultural approach to understanding teacher identity, agency and professional vulnerability in a context of secondary school reform. *Teaching and Teacher Education*, 21, 899–916. doi:10.1016/j.tate.2005.06.003.

Layard, R. and Dunn, J. (2009). *A good childhood: Searching for values in a competitive age.* London, England: Penguin Books.

Lazzari, A. (2014). Early childhood education and care in times of crisis. *European Early Childhood Education Research Journal*, 22, 4, 427–431. doi:10.1080/1350293X.2014.947829.

Lenz Taguchi, H. (2010). *Going beyond the theory/practice divide in early childhood education: Introducing an intra-active pedagogy.* London, England: Routledge.

Leseman, P.M. and Slot, P.L. (2014). Breaking the cycle of poverty: Challenges for European early childhood education and care. *European Early Childhood Education Research Journal*, 22, 3, 314–326. doi:10.1080/1350293X.2014.912894.

Lewis, M.G. (1993). *Without a word: Teaching beyond women's silence.* London, England: Routledge.

Little, H. and Eager, D. (2010). Risk, challenge and safety: Implications for play quality and playground design. *European Early Childhood Research Journal*, 18, 4, 497–513. doi: 10.1080/1350293X.2010.525949.

Løvgren, M. (2016). Emotional exhaustion in day-care workers. *European Early Childhood Education Research Journal*, 24, 1, 157–167. doi:10.1080/1350293X.2015.1120525.

MacNaughton, G. (2005). *Doing Foucault in early childhood studies: Applying a poststructural lens.* London, England: Routledge.

McCrea, K.T. (2014). Where's Beebee? The orphan crisis in global child welfare. In S.L. Witkin (Ed.) *Narrating social work through autoethnography* (pp. 25–65). New York, United States: Columbia University Press.

McGilchrist, I. (2009). *The master and his emissary.* London, England: Yale University Press.

McKendrick, J.H. (2011). What is life like for people experiencing poverty? In J.H. McKendrick, G. Mooney, J. Dickie and P. Kelly (Eds.) *Poverty in Scotland 2011: Towards a more equal society?* (pp. 111–130). London, England: CPAG.

McMillan, M. (1930). *The Nursery school.* London, England, Dent & Sons Ltd.

Mannion, G. (2007). Going spatial, going relational: Why "listening to children" and children's participation needs reframing. *Discourse: Studies in the Cultural Politics of Education*, 28, 3, 405–420. doi:10.1080/01596300701458970.

Marshall, K. (2006). Children's voices-early years. In Learning and Teaching Scotland: *Let's talk about listening to children: Towards a shared understanding for early years education in Scotland* (pp. 1–8). Glasgow, Scotland: Learning and Teaching Scotland.

Maynard, T., Waters, J. and Clement, J. (2013). Child-initiated learning, the outdoor environment and the 'underachieving' child. *Early Years: An International Research Journal.* 33, 3, 212–225. doi:10.1080/09575146.2013.771152.

Merleau-Ponty, M. (1962). *Phenomenology of perception.* London, England: Routledge and Kegan Paul.

Merleau-Ponty, M. (2008). *The world of perception* (Trans. O. Davis). Oxon, England: Routledge (Original work published 1948).

Miškolci, J. (2015). Dream interpretation as a component of researcher's reflexivity within an ethnographic research. *Ethnography and Education,* 10, 1, 76–91. doi:10.1080/ 17457823.2014.948563.

Moss, P. (2006). Listening to young children-beyond rights to ethics. In Learning and Teaching Scotland: *Let's talk about listening to children: Towards a shared understanding for early years education in Scotland* (pp. 17–23). Glasgow, Scotland: Learning and Teaching Scotland.

Moss, P. (2015). Time for more storytelling. *European Early Childhood Education Research Journal*, 23, 1, 1–4. doi:10.1080/1350293X.2014.991092.

Moss, P. and Petrie, P. (2002). *From children's services to children's spaces: Public policy, children and childhood*. London, England: RoutledgeFalmer.

Moyles, J. (2001). Passion, paradox and professionalism in early years education. *Early Years*, 21, 2, 81–95. doi:10.1080/09575140124792.

Muñoz, S.-A. (2009). *Children in the outdoors: A literature review*. Retrieved March 4, 2014 from www.playscotland.org/wp-content/uploads/assets/Children-Outdoors.pdf.

Murray, R. and O'Brien, L. (2005). 'Such enthusiasm — a joy to see': an evaluation of Forest School in England. Retrieved June 18, 2017 from: www.forestry.gov.uk/pdf/ForestSchoolEnglandReport.pdf/$file/ForestSchoolEnglandReport.pdf.

National Society for the Prevention of Cruelty to Children (2017). *Child Protection Plan and Register Statistics: 2012–2016*. Retrieved July 22, 2017 from: https://www.nspcc.org.uk/globalassets/documents/statistics-and-information/child-protection-register-statistics-united-kingdom.pdf.

Noddings, N. (1988). An ethic of care and its implications for instructional arrangements. *American Journal of Education*, 96, 2, 215–230. www.jstor.org/stable/1085252.

Noddings, N. (2003, 1984). *Caring: A feminine approach to ethics and moral education* (2nd ed.). London, England: University of California Press.

Noë, A. (2004). *Action in perception*. London, England: The MIT Press.

Nores, M. and Barnett, W.S. (2010). Benefits of early childhood interventions across the world: (Under) investing in the very young. *Economics of Education Review*, 29, 271–282. doi:10.1016/j.econedurev.2009.09.001.

Nutbrown, C. (1996). Wide eyes and open minds — Observing, assessing and respecting children's early achievements. In C. Nutbrown (Ed.) *Respectful educators-capable learners: Children's rights and early education* (pp. 44–55). London, England: Paul Chapman Publishing Limited.

Nutbrown, C. (2006). *Threads of thinking: Young children learning and the role of early education* (3rd ed.). London, England: SAGE Publications.

Nutbrown, C. (2011). A box of childhood: Small stories at the roots of a career. *International Journal of Early Years Education*, 19, 3–4, 233–248. doi:10.1080/09669760.2011.629491.

OECD (2006). *Starting Strong 11*. Retrieved December 12, 2012 from www.oecd.org/newsroom/37425999.pdf.

OECD (2007). *Reviews of national policies for education: Quality and equity of schooling in Scotland*. Retrieved December 12, 2012 from www.keepeek.com/Digital-Asset-Management/oecd/education/reviews-of-national-policies-for-education-scotland-2007_9789264041004-en.

O'Donohue, J. (1997). *Anam čara: Spiritual wisdom from the Celtic world*. London, England: Bantam Books.

O'Donohue, J. (2010). *The four elements: Reflections on nature*. London, England: Transworld Ireland.

Oliver, M. (2013). The social model of disability: Thirty years on. *Disability and Society*, 28, 7, 1024–1026. doi:10.1080/09687599.2013.818773.

Osgood, J. (2012). *Narratives from the nursery: Negotiating professional identities in early childhood*. London, England: Routledge.

Page, J. (2011). Do mothers want professionals to love their babies? *Journal of Early Childhood Research*, 9, 3, 310–323. doi:10.1177/1476718X11407980.

Page, J. (2013). Will the 'good' [working] mother please stand up? Professional and maternal concerns about education, care and love. *Gender and Education,* 25, 5, 548–563. doi:10.1080/09540253.2013.797069.

Page, J. and Elfer, P. (2013). The emotional complexity of attachment interactions in nursery. *European Early Childhood Education Research Journal,* 21, 4, 553–567. doi: 10.1080/1350293X.2013.766032.

Palmer, P.J. (2007). The courage to teach: Exploring the inner landscape of a teacher's life (Tenth anniversary ed.). San Francisco, United States: John Wiley and Sons.

Papatheodorou, T. (2009). Exploring relational pedagogy. In T. Papatheodorou and J. Moyles (Eds.) *Learning together in the early years: Exploring relational pedagogy* (pp. 3–17). Abingdon, England: Routledge.

Pelias, R.J. (2004). *A methodology of the heart: Evoking academic and daily life.* Oxford, England: Altamira Press.

Pelias, R.J. (2005). Performative writing as scholarship: An apology, an argument, an anecdote. *Cultural Studies ↔ Critical Methodologies,* 5, 4, 415–424. doi:10.1177/153270 8605279694.

Pelias, R.J. (2011). Writing into position: Strategies for composition and evaluation. In N.K. Denzin and Y.S. Lincoln (Eds.) *The SAGE handbook of qualitative research* (4th ed.). (pp. 659–668). London, England: SAGE.

Pelias, R.J. (2015). A story located in "shoulds": Toward a productive future for qualitative inquiry. *Qualitative Inquiry,* 21, 7, 609–611. doi:10.1177/1077800414555073.

Piaget, J. (1971). *Science of education and the psychology of the child.* London, England: Longman.

Piaget, J. (1973). *The child's conception of the world* (Trans. J. and A. Tomlinson). Herts, England: Paladin.

Ploder, A. and Stadlbauer, J. (2016). Strong reflexivity and its critics. Responses to autoethnography in German-speaking cultural and social sciences. *Qualitative Inquiry,* 22, 9, 753–765. doi:10.1177/1077800416658067.

Polkinghorne, D.E. (2007). Validity issues in narrative research. *Qualitative Inquiry,* 13, 471–486. doi:10.1177/1077800406297670.

Poulos, C.N. (2006). The ties that bind us, the shadows that separate us: Life and death, shadow and (dream) story. *Qualitative Inquiry,* 12, 1, 96–117. doi:10.1177/ 1077800405278780.

Reay, D. (2001). Finding or losing yourself? Working-class relationships to education. *Journal of Education Policy,* 16, 4, 333–346. doi:10.1080/02680930110054335.

Reed-Danahay, D.E. (1997). Introduction. In D.E. Reed-Danahay (Ed.) *Auto/Ethnography* (pp. 1–17). Oxford, England: Berg.

Rentzou, K. (2012). Examination of work environment factors relating to burnout syndrome of early childhood educators in Greece. *Child Care in Practice,* 18, 2, 165–181. doi:10.1080/13575279.2012.657609.

Riddell, S. (2009). Social justice, equality and inclusion in Scottish education. *Discourse: Studies in the Cultural Politics of Education,* 30, 3, 283–296. doi:10.1080/01596300903036889.

Riessman, C.K. (2008). *Narrative methods for the human sciences.* London, England: SAGE Publications.

Ruth, E. (1985). *Lamps of fire: Daily readings with St. John of the Cross.* London, England: Darton, Longman and Todd.

Sandelowski, M. (1994). The proof is in the pottery: Towards a poetic for qualitative inquiry. In J.M. Morse (Ed.) *Critical issues in qualitative research methods* (pp. 46–63). London, England: SAGE Publications.

Sandseter, E.B.H. (2009). Children's expressions of exhilaration and fear in risky play. *Contemporary Issues in Early Childhood,* 10, 2, 92–106. doi:10.2304/ciec.2009.10.2.92.

Schaefer, L., Downey, C.A. and Clandinin, D.J. (2014). Getting beyond elevator stories. In Clandinin, D.J., Schaefer, L. and Downey, C.A. (Eds.) *Narrative conceptions of knowledge: Towards understanding teacher attrition* (pp. 1–11). Bingley, United Kingdom: Emerald Group Publishing Ltd. Retrieved April 24, 2015 from http://dx.doi.org/10.1108/S1479-368720140000023001.

Schreyer, I. and Krause, M. (2016). Pedagogical staff in children's day care centres in Germany: Links between working conditions, job satisfaction, commitment and work-related stress. *Early Years*, 36, 2, 132–147. doi:10.1080/09575146.2015.1115390.

Schweinhart, L.J. (2013). Long-term follow-up of a preschool experiment. *Journal of Experimental Criminology*, 9, 389–409. doi:10.1007/s11292-013-9190-3.

Scottish Executive (1995). *The Children (Scotland) Act: Regulations and guidance, volume 1: Support and protection for children and their families.* Retrieved May 10, 2015 from www.gov.scot/Publications/2004/10/20066/44708.

Scottish Executive (2001). *For Scotland's children.* Edinburgh, Scotland: Scottish Executive. Retrieved November 12, 2012 from www.scotland.gov.uk/Resource/Doc/1141/0105219.pdf.

Scottish Executive (2004a). *A guide for parents: The Education (Additional Support for Learning) (Scotland) Act 2004* (2nd ed.). Retrieved April 9, 2015 from www.gov.scot/Resource/Doc/47251/0023727.pdf.

Scottish Executive (2004b). *Getting it right for every child: Consultation pack on the review of the children's hearing system.* Edinburgh, Scotland: Scottish Executive.

Scottish Government (2008a). *Early years and early intervention: A joint Scottish Government and COSLA policy statement.* Edinburgh, Scotland: Scottish Government. Retrieved February 3, 2015 from www.gov.scot/Resource/Doc/215889/0057733.pdf.

Scottish Government (2008b). *The early years framework.* Edinburgh, Scotland: Scottish Government. Retrieved June 18, 2017 from: http://www.gov.scot/Resource/Doc/257007/0076309.pdf.

Scottish Government (2010). *Pre-birth to three: Positive outcomes for children and families.* Edinburgh, Scotland: Scottish Government. Retrieved April 30, 2012 from www.educationscotland.gov.uk/Images/PreBirthToThreeBooklet_tcm4-633448.pdf.

Scottish Government (2011). *Early years framework: Progress so far.* Edinburgh, Scotland: Scottish Government. Retrieved May 4, 2012 from www.scotland.gov.uk/Publications/2011/01/13114328/14.

Scottish Government (2012). *Getting it right for every child: A guide to getting it right for every child.* Edinburgh, Scotland: Scottish Government. Retrieved February 4, 2013 from www.scotland.gov.uk/gettingitright.

Scottish Government (2014a). *Children and Young People (Scotland) Act 2014: Early learning and childcare: Statutory guidance.* Retrieved June 12, 2015 from www.gov.scot/Resource/0045/00457025.pdf.

Scottish Government (2014b). *Children's social work statistics Scotland, 2012–2013.* Retrieved 10 July, 2015 from www.gov.scot/Resource/0044/00447448.pdf.

Scottish Government (2015). *Child safety and wellbeing-child protection: Child protection key trends.* Retrieved June 12, 2015 from www.gov.scot/Topics/Statistics/Browse/Children/TrendChildProtection.

Scottish Government and the Poverty Truth Commission (2015). *Poverty in Scotland.* Retrieved June 10, 2015 from www.gov.scot/Resource/0048/00480340.pdf.

Semetsky, I. (2012). Living, learning, loving: Constructing a new ethics of integration in education. *Discourse: Studies in the Cultural Politics of Education*, 33, 1, 47–59. doi:10.1080/01596306.2012.632163.

Sermijn, J., Devlieger, P. and Loots, G. (2008). The narrative construction of the self: Selfhood as rhizomatic story. *Qualitative Inquiry*, 14, 4, 632–650. doi:10.1177/1077800408314356.

Sheets-Johnstone, M. (2003). Child's play: A multidisciplinary perspective. *Human Studies*, 26, 409–430.

Siraj-Blatchford, I., Mayo, A., Melhuish, E., Taggart, B., Sammons, P. and Sylva, K. (2011). *Performing against the odds: Developmental trajectories of children in the EPPSE 3–16 study.* Retrieved April 12, 2012 from www.education.gov.uk/publications/standard/publicationDetail/Page1/DFE-RR128.

Smith, P. (2013). This closet. In P. Smith (Ed.) *Both sides of the table: Autoethnographies of educators learning and teaching with/in [dis]ability* (pp. 103–117). Oxford, England: Peter Lang.

Smyth, J. and McInerney, P. (2013). Whose side are you on? Advocacy ethnography: Some methodological aspects of narrative portraits of disadvantaged young people, in socially critical research. *International Journal of Qualitative Studies in Education*, 26, 1, 1–20. doi:10.1080/09518398.2011.604649.

Smyth, J. and McInerney, P. (2014). 'Ordinary kids' navigating geographies of educational opportunity in the context of an Australian 'place based intervention'. *Journal of Education Policy,* 29, 3, 285–301. doi:10.1080/02680939.2013.794304.

Soanes, C. and Stevenson, A. (2008). *Concise Oxford English Dictionary* (11th ed.). Oxford, England: Oxford University Press.

Sparkes, A.C. (2009). Novel ethnographic representations and the dilemmas of judgement. *Ethnography and Education*, 4, 3, 301–319. doi:10.1080/17457820903170119.

Sparkes, A.C. (2013). Autoethnography: Self-indulgent or something more? In P. Sikes (Ed.) *Autoethnography, Volume 1* (pp. 175–194). London, England: SAGE.

Sparkes, A.C. and Smith, B. (2009). Judging the quality of qualitative inquiry: Criteriology and relativism in action. *Psychology of Sport and Exercise*, 10, 491–497. doi:10.1016/j.pschsport.2009.02.006.

Spry, T. (2001). Performing autoethnography: An embodied methodological praxis. *Qualitative Inquiry*, 7, 6, 706–732.

Spry, T. (2011a). Performative autoethnography: Critical embodiments and possibilities. In N.K. Denzin and Y.S. Lincoln (Eds.) *The SAGE handbook of qualitative research* (4th ed.) (pp. 497–511). London, England: SAGE.

Spry, T. (2011b). The accusing body. *Cultural Studies ↔ Critical Methodologies*, 11, 4, 410–414. doi:10.1177/1532708611414675.

St. Pierre, E.A. (2011). Post qualitative research: The critique and coming after. In N.K. Denzin and Y.S. Lincoln (Eds.) *The SAGE handbook of qualitative research* (4th ed.) (pp. 611–625). London, England: SAGE.

Stephenson, A. (2003). Physical risk-taking: Dangerous or endangered? *Early Years: An International Research Journal*, 23, 1, 35–43. doi:10.1080/0957514032000045573.

Sumsion, J. (2001). Workplace violence in early childhood settings: A counter-narrative. *Contemporary Issues in Early Childhood*, 2, 195–207.

Sumsion, J. (2004). Early childhood teachers' constructions of their resilience and thriving: A continuing investigation. *International Journal of Early Years Education*, 12, 3, 275–290. doi:10.1080/0966976042000268735.

Sylva, K., Melhuish, E., Sammons, P., Siraj-Blatchford, I. and Taggart, B. (2004). The effective provision of pre-school education (EPPE) project: Final report. London, England: DfES. Retrieved June 17, 2017 from http://eprints.ioe.ac.uk/5309/1/sylva2004EPPEfinal.pdf.

Taggart, G. (2016). Compassionate pedagogy: The ethics of care in early childhood professionalism. *European Early Childhood Education Research Journal*, 24, 2, 173–185. doi: 10.1080/1350293X.2014.970847.

Thewless, J. (2009). *Unpublished collection of private poetry.*

Thewless, J. (2016). *Unpublished collection of private poetry.*

Todd, S. (2015). Between body and spirit: The liminality of pedagogical relationships. In M. Griffiths, M.H. Hoveid, S. Todd and C. Winter (Eds.) *Re-imagining relationships in education: Ethics, politics and practices* (pp. 56–72). West Sussex, United Kingdom: Wiley Blackwell.

Trevarthen, C. (2012). Finding a place with meaning in a busy human world: How does the story begin, and who helps? *European Early Childhood Education Research Journal*, 20, 3, 303–312. doi:10.1080/1350293X.2012.704757.

Tsai, M.-L. (2007). Understanding young children's personal narratives: What I have learned from young children's sharing time narratives in a Taiwanese kindergarten classroom. In D.J. Clandinin (Ed.) *Handbook of narrative inquiry: Mapping a methodology* (pp. 461–488). London, England: SAGE.

Tuan, Y-F. (1977). *Space and place: The perspective of experience.* London, England: Edward Arnold.

United Nations (1989). *The convention on the rights of the child.* New York, United States: United Nations.

Uotinen, J. (2011). Senses, bodily knowledge, and autoethnography: Unbeknown knowledge form and ICU experience. *Qualitative Health Research*, 21, 10, 1307–1315. doi:10.1177/1049732311413908.

Vandenbroeck, M. (2014). The brainification of early childhood education and other challenges to academic rigour. *European Early Childhood Education Research Journal*, 22, 1, 1–3. doi:10.1080/1350293X.2013.868206.

Van Laere, K., Vandenbroeck, M., Roet, G. and Peeters, J. (2014). Challenging the feminisation of the workforce: Rethinking the mind-body dualism in early childhood education and care. *Gender and Education*, 26, 3, 232–245. doi:10.1080/09540253. 2014.901721.

Varela, F.J. (1999). *Ethical know-how: Action, wisdom, and cognition.* Stanford, United States: Stanford University Press.

Verducci, S. (2014). Introduction: Narratives in ethics of education. *Studies in Philosophy of Education*, 33, 575–585. doi:10.1007/s11217-014-9411-x.

Vogt, F. (2002). A caring teacher: Explorations into primary school teacher's professional identity and ethic of care. *Gender and Education*, 14, 3, 251–264. doi:10.1080/095402 5022000010712.

Vygotsky, L. and Luria, A. (1994). Tool and symbol in child development. In R. van der Veer and J. Valsiner (Eds.) *The Vygotsky Reader* (Trans. T. Prout and R. van der Veer) (pp. 99–174). Oxford, England: Blackwell Ltd.

Warren, J. (2011). Reflexive teaching: Toward critical autoethnographic practices of/ in/on pedagogy. *Cultural Studies ↔ Critical Methodologies*, 11, 2, 139–144. doi: 10.1177/1532708611401332.

Watkins, M. (2010). Desiring recognition, accumulating affect. In M. Gregg and G.J. Seigworth (Eds.) *The affect theory reader* (pp. 269–285). London, England: Duke University Press.

Watkins, M. (2011). Teacher's tears and affective geography of the classroom. *Emotion, Space and Society*, 4, 137–143. doi:10.1016/j.emposa.2010.03.001.

Webb, D. (2010). Paulo Freire and 'the need for a kind of education in hope'. *Cambridge Journal of Education*, 40, 4, 327–339. doi:10.1080/0305764X.2010.526591.

Wedge, P. and Prosser, H. (1973). *Born to fail?* London, England: Arrow Books Limited.

White, J. (2008). *Playing and learning outdoors: Making provision for high-quality experiences in the outdoor environment.* Oxon, England: Routledge.

Whitty, G. (2001). Education, social class and social exclusion. *Journal of Education Policy,* 16, 4, 287–295. doi:10.1080/02680930110054308.

Witherell, C. and Noddings, N. (1991). Prologue: An invitation to our readers. In C. Witherell and N. Noddings (Eds.) *Stories lives tell: Narrative and dialogue in education* (pp. 1–12). London, England: Teachers College Press.

Witkin, S.L. (2014a) Autoethnography: The opening act. In S.L. Witkin (Ed.). *Narrating social work through autoethnography* (pp. 1–24). New York, United States: Columbia University Press.

Witkin, S.L. (2014b). Reality isn't what it used to be: An inquiry of transformative change. In S.L. Witkin (Ed.) *Narrating social work through autoethnography* (pp. 284–315). New York, United States: Columbia University Press.

Zembylas, M. (2004). The emotional characteristics of teaching: An ethnographic study of one teacher. *Teaching and Teacher Education,* 20, 185–201. doi:10.1016/j.tate.2003.09.008.

Zembylas, M. (2005). Discursive practices, genealogies, and emotional rules: A post-structuralist view on emotion and identity in teaching. *Teaching and Teacher Education,* 21, 935–948. doi:10.1016/j.tate.2005.06.005.

Zembylas, M. (2007). Emotional capital and education: Theoretical insights from Bourdieu. *British Journal of Educational Studies,* 55, 4, 443–463. doi:10.1111/j.1467-8527.2007.00390.x.

INDEX